MW01329671

THE LUMINOUS MOONS:
THE PROPHETIC BIOGRAPHY

The Luminous Moons

THE LIGHT OF THE AZHAR

Shaykh Salih al-Ja'fari

Imam Ghazali INSTITUTE

LIGHT of the AZHAR

ISBN: 978-1-8384776-2-2 (Hardback) | 979-8-3542689-7-9 (Amazon)

Translation, proofreading & editing: Mohammed A Shamsudoha and Ahmad Muhammad
Typesetting & Cover design: Imran Rahim, Etherea Design

Proudly printed in the USA.

Exclusively distributed by Imam Ghazali Publishing, New Jersey, USA.
Managed by Sattaur Publishing Group.

info@imamghazalipublishing.com
www.imamghazalipublishing.com

Contents

	PREFACE	1
	FOREWORD	3
	BIOGRAPHY	8
CHAPTER 1	Introduction	16
CHAPTER 2	The Best of Allāh's Creation ﷺ	20
CHAPTER 3	That He is Nūr (Light) ﷺ	24
CHAPTER 4	His Spiritual Lights ﷺ	30
CHAPTER 5	Preservation of His Lineage ﷺ and the Transference of the Muḥammadan Light ﷺ	34
CHAPTER 6	When His Mother Conceived Him ﷺ	40
CHAPTER 7	Concerning His Birth ﷺ	44
CHAPTER 8	His Muʿjiza (miracles) on the Night He Was Born ﷺ	50
CHAPTER 9	His Nursing ﷺ	52
CHAPTER 10	The Expansion of His Noble Chest ﷺ	54
CHAPTER 11	Earning a Livelihood and Marriage	58
CHAPTER 12	Placing of the Black Stone in the Sacred House	62
CHAPTER 13	Beginning of Revelation	66
CHAPTER 14	Isrāʾ and Mi'raaj	70

CHAPTER 15 His ﷺ Hijra (Migration) 78
CHAPTER 16 Entry into al-Madīna al-Munawwara 80
CHAPTER 17 Expeditions and the Conquest of Makka 84
CHAPTER 18 Concerning His Physical Appearance 88
CHAPTER 19 His ﷺ Lofty Character 96
CHAPTER 20 Seeking Means Through him ﷺ 100
CHAPTER 21 Regarding the Life of Rasul Allāh ﷺ after His Departure from this World 110
CHAPTER 22 Concerning some of His ﷺ Miracles (Muʿjizāt) 118
CHAPTER 23 Concerning His Love ﷺ 128
CHAPTER 24 Visiting Him ﷺ at His Noble Rawda in Madīna 132
CHAPTER 25 The Following of the Four Imāms 142
CHAPTER 26 Closing Duʿā 146

APPENDICES
Appendix 1 157
Appendix 2 161

Preface

In the name of Allāh

All praise belongs to Allāh, by Whose Grace good works are accomplished.

And we ask Allāh ﷻ to send prayers and peace on the one who was sent as a mercy to all the worlds, the Master of the First ones and the Last ones, Sayyiduna Muḥammad, and upon his family, and all his Companions, and those who followed them with excellence until the Day of Judgement.

And may Allāh be pleased with our Shaykhs, Sayyidi Shaykh Ṣāliḥ al-Jaʿfarī and Sayyidi Shaykh ʿAbd al-Ghani Ṣāliḥ al-Jaʿfarī.

To proceed: The scholars have been honored with the writing of the blessed Prophetic biography ﷺ because of what it contains of wisdom and lessons. For example, Shaykh al-Barzanji ؓ wrote a Prophetic biography ﷺ and named it *ʿIqd al-Jawhar fi Mawlid al-Nabi al-Azhar* (The Jewelled Necklace of the Resplendent Prophet's Birth) and it is commonly known as the Mawlid al-Barzanji. Sayyid Muḥammad ʿUthmān Sirr al-Khatm, one of the students of Sidi Aḥmad b. Idrīs ؓ, wrote a Prophetic biography ﷺ, *al-Asrar al-Rabbaniyya*, which is known as the Mawlid al-Uthmani. These books are written in such a beautiful way that no one is able to achieve this except for those who have mastery in the Arabic language and have abundant knowledge of the religious sciences. As our Shaykh, Sayyidi Ṣāliḥ al-Ja'farī ﷺ is from the greatest of the scholars of his time, and the most eloquent of the poets of his era, he did not hesitate in giving us something like this and wrote for us a Prophetic, Muḥammadan biography ﷺ and named it *al-Aqmār al-Nūrāniyya* (The Luminous Moons).

In its introduction he wrote that he saw Sayyiduna Jibrīl ﷺ and asked him for his supplication. He ﷺ replied to him, "May Allāh complete it (*al-Aqmar al-Nūrāniyya*)," and verily Allāh completed it for him!

This is the first edition of this blessed work in the English language, which the sons of the Ja'fariyya Aḥmadiyya Muḥammadiyya Ṭariqa from the United Kingdom and the United States of America have completed in a wonderful, collective effort. I ask Allāh that He places this work on their scale of good deeds inshaAllāh, and I ask the Lord ﷻ that He benefits [by it] everyone who reads it. This work also contains a foreword from the eminent teacher, [Shaykh] Dr. Fathi Hijazi, a professor at al-Azhar University, for which we thank his eminence for his generous participation in this work.

MUḤAMMAD ṢĀLIḤ B. 'ABD AL-GHANI B. ṢĀLIḤ AL-JA'FARĪ
Shaykh of the Ja'fariyya Tariqa in Egypt and the Islamic World

Foreword

In the name of Allah, Most Gracious, Most Merciful

Praise belongs to Allah alone, as befitting the majesty of His Countenance, the magnificence of His Might, and His Ample Blessings, as many times as all that is contained in the knowledge of Allah (Majestic is He in His Exaltedness).

And peace, prayers and blessings be upon the Best of Allah's Creation, His beloved and chosen one, our Master and Liege, Muhammad, the one sent with dazzling verses and radiant lights, and upon his pure family, righteous Companions and the outstanding followers. O Allah! Make us from them by Your grace and generosity, O Most Generous! Ameen.

To proceed: Our Master Muhammad (may the peace and blessings of Allah be upon him and his family) is the Mercy of the Worlds because he is upon an exalted standard of character. His Lord raised him and took charge of him throughout his entire life in order that he become an eternal light, and a mercy for all the slaves of Allah, in all aspects. As such, he is honored by his beautiful life (*sira*), by which he became a role model for the wayfarers to Allah, and a lighthouse for every god-fearing person and those who desire the gardens of delight, and the felicity of this life and the Hereafter. Likewise, those who follow him from his family under the banner of the Master of the First and the Last.

Scholars have written his biography since the time of his Companions till this day of ours and will continue to do so till the Day of Judgment, with the hope that it to be a good act that they have carried out for themselves by which they will meet their Lord, "The day on which no soul shall control anything for (another) soul, and the command on that day shall be entirely Allah's."[1]

From those scholars in our present time, is our teacher and shaykh, *Salih al-Ja'fari* – may Allah be pleased with him and please him, and bestow vast mercy upon him. He used to always speak about the Prophet's life (may the peace and blessings of Allah be upon him and his family), and then he wrote his ﷺ biography in a summarized form for people of all levels, titled: "*Al-Sira al-Nabawiyya al-Muhammadiyya – al-Mawlid al-Ja'fari*" [The Prophetic Muhammadan Biography – the *Ja'fari* Mawlid] and it's known as "*al-Aqmar al-Nuraniyya*" [the Luminous Moons].

I knew our Shaykh *al-Ja'fari* in the last ten years of his life, in noble knowledge. We recognized in him subtle knowledge, radiant and sublime light, and love for the Master of Messengers. His chain of transmission is well known to all, in the canonical recitations of the Qur'an, Exegesis, Hadith, books of Sacred Law, Arabic, Foundational Principles (*uṣūl*) and Islamic history. We saw that he has clear insight on life and people, the former of them and the latter of them. He has a remaining legacy amongst the people until the Day of Judgment, and for that, his concise words were in need of commentary and clarification. For this reason he would persist in giving lessons regularly. When he sat to give a lesson in the courtyard of Masjid al-Azhar at *dhuhr*, he would not get up until '*asr*, and it was like that in all his lessons. In fact, I heard from him, while sitting in his daily Ramadan lessons, that at time of the

1 Al-Infitar, 19

commemoration of his grandfather al-Husayn ﵁, he would sit and give lessons from *dhuhr* until the break of dawn [*fajr*], not getting up except for prayer, and then return. That is how it was for the whole week, "That is the grace of Allah which He gives to whom He pleases and Allah is the Lord of tremendous grace."

For that reason, it is good for our sons [and daughters] in all countries to take his spoken and written words with due earnestness and diligence, seeking benefit and guidance along with every slave of Allah. Allah is the ultimate objective, and He is the Guide to the straight path.

I surely give thanks to Allah the Generous who has enabled the sons [and daughters] of the Muslims to benefit from the works of the righteous.

May Allah bestow blessings upon our Master and Liege, Muhammad, the Harbinger of Glad Tidings and the Warner, and upon his Companions and the followers. And all praise belongs to Allah, the Lord of the Worlds,

Written by the one hoping for the pardon of his Lord,

DR. FATHI ʿABD AL-RAHMAN HIJAZI AL-AZHARI
Faculty of Arabic Language,
The Noble Azhar University, Cairo, Egypt

Biography

Birth

Shaykh Ṣāliḥ al-Jaʿfarī ﵁ was born on the 15th Jumāda al-Thānī 1328 AH (24th June 1910 CE) in the town of Dongola, Sudan.

Noble Lineage

He is the descendant of al-Sayyid ʿAlī al-Hādī ﵁, b. al-Sayyid Muḥammad al-Jawād ﵁, b. al-Sayyid ʿAlī al-Riḍā ﵁, b. al-Sayyid Mūsā al-Kāẓim ﵁, b. al-Sayyid Jaʿfar al-Ṣādiq ﵁, b. al-Sayyid Muḥammad al-Bāqir ﵁, b. al-Sayyid al-Imām ʿAlī Zayn al-Ābidīn ﵁, b. Mawlānā al-Imām al-Ḥusayn ﵁, b. al-Imām ʿAlī ﵁, the husband of the pure lady Sayyida Fāṭima al-Zahrāʾ ﵂, the daughter of our Prophet and beloved, Sayyiduna Muḥammad ﷺ.

Early Life

The Shaykh was brought up in Dongola, where he was raised with a religious and spiritual upbringing, filled with the obedience of Allāh Most High, and a deep love of the Messenger of Allāh ﷺ. His noble family was famous for its learning, piety, righteousness, generosity and the study of the noble Qurʾān and the noble sciences of the religion. The grandfather of Shaykh Ṣāliḥ, after whom he was named (Shaykh Ṣāliḥ al-Rifāʿī ﵁) was one of the hardworking scholars of al-Azhar. After emigrating from Egypt to Dongola, he established circles for the memorization of the noble Qurʾān and gatherings for teaching beneficial knowledge in the Grand Mosque [of Dongola]. He would devote his heart and mind, and his entire body to knowledge and the Qurʾān. Shaykh Ṣāliḥ al-Jaʿfarī inherited from his grandfather the love of knowledge, worship, and turning away from the adornments of the worldly life. At the age of fourteen, Shaykh Ṣāliḥ memorized the Qurʾān with its rules and different recitation styles at the hands of Shaykh ʿAlī Abū ʿAwf al-Sanhūrī and Sayyid Ḥasan Effendī, both of whom memorized it with his grandfather. Shaykh Ṣāliḥ also studied Mālikī fiqh with Shaykh ʿAlī Muḥammad Jawwī, one of the scholars of al-Azhar and the Imām of the Grand Mosque of Dongola.

Shaykh Ṣāliḥ's father was Sayyid Muḥammad Ṣāliḥ, who was known for his hardworking attitude and responsibility towards taking care of both his immediate and extended family. During the night, he would stand in worship of his Lord until the time nearing dawn; after which he would go to the Grand Mosque, open the door, and light the lamps. He would wait until the worshippers would come and then perform the Adhān for the Fajr prayer, and then lead the prayer. After that, he would return home and wake his family up to pray before sunrise. Sayyid Muḥammad Ṣāliḥ was a strong and active man, and he did not like to see people being lazy. His farm was one of the best in Dongola, and he was known in his city as 'The Lion' because of his strength and intensity in work. He performed the Ḥajj ten times and would serve the pilgrims, take care of their needs, and would carry weapons in order to defend against robbers and bandits that would steal goods from the pilgrims on the Ḥajj route. He would travel from Sudan to Egypt to visit his forefathers from the Ahl al-Bayt and the resting places of the saints and scholars. He would also visit his son Shaykh Ṣaliḥ in al-Azhar. These pure characteristics show the purity of this noble lineage. Sayyid Muḥammad Ṣāliḥ remained persistent in prayer and worship, consistently performing his prayers in congregation and always making sure that he would be in the first row throughout his life.

Journey to al-Azhar for Knowledge

Shaykh Ṣāliḥ al-Jaᶜfarī spent his youth studying various sciences of Islamic knowledge until the time came for him to travel to al-Azhar. An indication came from Shaykh ᶜAbd al-ᶜĀlī b. Sayyid Aḥmad b. Idrīs ﷺ, which was the cause for his firm resolve and decision to travel. Shaykh Ṣāliḥ says, "Before I arrived at al-Azhar, one of my townspeople brought the first volume of al-Nawawī's commentary on Ṣaḥīḥ Muslim. I borrowed it from him and began to read it diligently. I saw Shaykh ᶜAbd al-ᶜĀlī al-Idrīsī ﷺ in a vision, sitting on a chair with provisions for travel around him. I heard someone say "The shaykh wants to travel to al-Azhar in Egypt." I went and greeted him, and kissed his hand. He said to me with all seriousness, "Knowledge is taken from the hearts of men, not from books!" He repeated that and then I woke from my sleep – my Lord had inspired me to travel to al-Azhar." Shaykh Ṣāliḥ was directed towards al-Azhar to study with the scholars in their gatherings, because of the science and the knowledge it contains, which can hardly be found elsewhere – it gathered all the sciences. Shaykh Ṣāliḥ says in one of his books that he saw Shaykh Aḥmad b. Idrīs ﷺ saying to him in a vision, "Allāh is with you. Study fiqh according to the four schools." Shaykh Ṣāliḥ said, "When I awoke, I told one of my teachers of this vision and he said, 'If this vision is true, then its interpretation is that you should travel to al-Azhar – where fiqh is taught according to the four schools'". Allāh fulfilled this vision!

Shaykh Ṣāliḥ continued and said, "And when I reached al-Azhar, I found the ḥadith scholar Shaykh Muḥammad Ibrāhīm al-Samaluti ﷺ, teaching al-Nawawī's commentary on Sahih Muslim, so I sat down to listen to him, and heard him teaching the ḥadith: "There is no hijra after the Opening of Makka, but only Jiḥad and intention. When you are called upon to go, then go forth!".

When Shaykh Ṣāliḥ reached Egypt, he joined al-Azhar and remained there completely. It was for the sake of seeking knowledge that he left his country and homeland, leaving his family and children, so he would not waste even a moment in something other than gaining knowledge or benefiting from the great scholars of al-Azhar at that time. He completed his studies with sincerity and dedication, and received the Alimiyya certificate, the highest degree from al-Azhar (12 year program), according to its old system. Later, when al-Azhar began to reorganize their education system, and develop specialisms and set up different faculties, Shaykh Ṣāliḥ attended the Faculty of Sharīʿa, where he obtained another degree, not out of necessity but from love for knowledge. The diligent student would only leave al-Azhar to visit his grandfather, Imām al-Husayn ﷺ and the Ahl al-Bayt ﷺ.

Becoming a teacher and the Imām at al-Azhar

Shaykh Ṣāliḥ did not restrict himself to only the obligations of his job. Rather, he taught and gave sermons in all corners of al-Azhar. Hearts rushed towards him because of the beneficial knowledge Allāh had bestowed upon him, and his sincere and truthful advice. Students came from both inside and outside al-Azhar, such that some of those working with him at al-Azhar began to complain because of the Shaykh's stepping forward to teach and lecture, envying his acceptance among people. This continued until an opportunity came for the Shaykh to display the breadth of his knowledge and suitability for such a great place – whereby objectors submitted, arguers were silenced, and lovers of the Shaykh made happy. This opportunity arose after the passing of one of his teachers, the erudite scholar Shaykh Yūsuf al-Dijwī ﵀ (d.1365 AH–1946 CE). The Scholars and students of al-Azhar gathered to bid farewell to their great teacher. Shaykh Dr. Muḥammad Rajab al-Bayūmī ﵀, the renowned teacher of literature and rhetoric at al-Azhar, relates the story:

> One of the situations in which the magnificence of Shaykh Ṣāliḥ reached a peak was in his eulogy of his great teacher Shaykh Yūsuf al-Dijwī ﵀. I was a student in the Faculty of Arabic Language when the shaykh's passing was announced along with the time of his funeral prayer. I rushed quickly to bid the shaykh farewell, and the event was incredibly moving. In front was a group of the great and senior scholars, led by Shaykh Muṣṭafā ʿAbd al-Razzāq ﵀ (Shaykh al-Azhar, d.1366 AH-1947 CE). When the procession reached its end at the grave, Shaykh Ṣāliḥ stood to give a speech eulogizing his teacher. He began by drawing on the words of the Messenger of Allāh ﷺ, 'Allāh does not take away knowledge by taking it away from the people, but takes it away by the death of the scholars, until none of them remain, and people will take ignorant leaders, who when consulted, answer without knowledge. So, they will go astray and will lead the people astray.

Then Shaykh Ṣāliḥ began to explain the great rank of the deceased scholar, praising his stance against the innovators and atheists. The magnanimity of the scene, the tremendousness of the occasion, and the gathering of people were things that would make the soul and speech of the eulogiser expand greatly and flow beautifully, pouring forth with emotion and excitement. His voice contained a sadness that moved the souls of those listening and swept their hearts away. The speaker had barely finished his eulogy before the Shaykh of al-Azhar asked about him in amazement and quickly rushed to appoint him as a teacher in al-Azhar. His official appointment gave him a stability that muted those who criticised the advancement of the shaykh because of their own envy, considering him to transgress the bounds of someone in his situation when he began to give daily sermons without tiring. These people were a minority, though, and came to know of their mistake and submitted to the truth after their defiance." (Majallah al-Azhar, p.1874, Shawwāl 1399 AH – September 1979 CE).

The Friday Lessons at al-Azhar

Shaykh Ṣāliḥ held a lesson after the Friday prayer in al-Azhar. This lesson was a religious and spiritual school unto itself, with its ilm taken from the Qur᾽ān, the Sunna, and the Sharīʿa. And it was infused with the spirituality of Sufism and its spiritual upbringing, so that it revealed the Sufi truths. He poured from himself into his lessons with īmān from his soul, so that the purity of asceticism, piety, and righteousness appeared, and the lights of guidance shined, and the purity of the fiṭra showed. The Shaykh would welcome questions and answer them with patience, love and gentleness. He delivered these answers in a way that was readily received and easy to understand for the listeners, and this, coupled with his mastery of the sciences, attracted masses of people from different facets of society.

His Passing ﵀ and Legacy

Shaykh Ṣāliḥ al-Jaʿfarī spent his life in the constant remembrance of Allāh ﷻ, calling and guiding people to Him ﷻ and in following the Sunna of Prophet ﷺ. He returned to his Lord, well-pleased and well-pleasing, on 18th Jumāda al-Awwal 1399 AH (16th April 1979 CE) and is buried next to his mosque in Darrāsa, Cairo. Shaykh Ṣāliḥ would often come to this very place as a student, to read and memorize various works that he was studying and would refer to it as the 'Garden of the ever-living ones'. Students of al-Azhar flock to his maqam, to memorize the Qur'ān, the books of the Sunna, and primary texts in the religious sciences, because of this blessing of Shaykh Ṣāliḥ. He said, "My path is the Qur'ān, (the seeking and application of beneficial) knowledge and God-consciousness, and praising the Messenger of Allāh, the eraser of all misguidance." The Shaykh has a beautiful legacy of published works and an established spiritual path, which has disciples and students all over the world, from the Middle East, Malaysia, North Africa, India, Nigeria, South Africa, North America and Europe. Many of the senior scholars of al-Azhar today, were students of Shaykh Ṣāliḥ, and they often cite him in their lessons. Some of these scholars include Shaykh Dr. ʿĀlī Gomaa (the former Grand Mufti of Egypt), Shaykh Dr. Fatḥī Hijāzī (Senior Professor at the Faculty of Arabic Language at al-Azhar University) and the late Shaykh Dr. Aḥmad Ṭāḥā Rayyān ﵀ (the Head of the Mālikī Scholars of Egypt, d. 2021 CE). The late son of Shaykh Ṣāliḥ, Shaykh ʿAbd al-Ghanī al-Jaʿfarī ﵀, established many masājid across Egypt, which in addition to being centers (sāḥat, lit. courtyards) for the spiritual path of his father (al-Ṭarīqa al-Jaʿfarīyya), offer bakeries, libraries, hospitals, pharmacies, Qur'ān memorization schools and adult learning classes – all of which are free to those unable to pay. These centers, including the principal center in Darrāsa, Cairo, host twice weekly gatherings of Qurʾān recitation, lessons of religious and spiritual knowledge, dhikr, ṣalawāt and praise of the Prophet ﷺ and the Ahl al-Bayt عليهم السلام in the form of madīḥ, taken from the 12 volume collection that Shaykh Ṣāliḥ wrote, known as the Dīwān al-Jaʿfarī.

How fitting it is that Shaykh Ṣāliḥ al-Jaʿfarī is buried near his grandfather, Imām al-Ḥusayn عليه السلام and al-Azhar al-Sharīf! May Allāh ﷻ illuminate his grave and make it a garden from the gardens of Paradise. May he drink from the hand of the one he loved ﷺ, and enter the highest Paradise, holding his blessed and noble hand ﷺ, alongside all his family, teachers, disciples, students and those who loved him. Āmīn.

The Luminous Moons

THE LIGHT OF THE AZHAR

Shaykh Salih al-Ja'fari

Imam Ghazali INSTITUTE

LIGHT of the AZHAR

CHAPTER 1

Introduction

All praises belong to Allāh, the One who has honored the universe by manifesting the best of creation ﷺ, who dispelled by his *Shari'a*, the darkness of polytheism and invited the creation to the worship of his Master, Allāh.

I bear witness that there is none worthy of worship, besides Allāh alone, who has no partner, free from pre-Islāmic beliefs. I bear witness that our master Muḥammad ﷺ is His beloved and chosen one.

I, the poor humble servant, who hopes for the mercy of his beneficent Lord, Ṣāliḥ al-Ja'farī al-Ḥusaynī, the son of Muḥammad b. Ṣāliḥ al-Ja'farī, whose family lineage goes up to Sayyid Ja'far al-Ṣādiq ؓ, says:

I am a student of the one possessing gnosis and guidance to the *Aḥmadiyya* and *Khātmiyya* path, Sayyid Muḥammad al-Sharīf b. Sayyid 'Abd al-'Ālī b. Sayyid Aḥmad b. Idrīs, may Allāh be pleased with them all, perpetually by the number of those who adopt their path and find the sweetness of their litanies and recite them.

And I am the student of Shaykh Ḥabīb Allāh al-Shinqīṭī in the sciences and ḥadith, and the student of Shaykh Muḥammad Ibrāhīm al-Muḥaddith, Shaykh Muḥammad Bakhīt al-Muṭī'ī, Shaykh Yūsuf al-Dijwī, Shaykh Maḥmūd al-Ghunaymī and other senior scholars of the noble Azhar. May Allāh send vast mercy upon all of them, that will continue and remain from His grace.

الفصل الأول

المُقَدِّمَة

الْحَمْدُ لِلّٰهِ الَّذِى شَرَّفَ الأَكْوَانَ بِظُهورِ خَيْرِ البَرِيَّةِ ، فَأَزَالَ بِشَرْعِهِ ظُلْمَةَ الشِّرْكِ، وَدَعَا الْخَلَائِقَ إِلَى عِبادَةِ مَوْلَاهُ ، وَأَشْهَدُ أَنْ لَا إِلَهَ إِلَّا اللهُ وَحْدَهُ لَا شَرِيكَ لَهُ ، تَنَزَّهَ عَنْ عَقَائِدِ الْجَاهِلِيَّةِ ، وَأَشْهَدُ أَنَّ سَيِّدَنَا مُحَمَّداً حَبِيبَهُ وَمُصْطَفَاهُ ،

وَبَعْدُ :فَيَقُولُ العَبْدُ الفَقِيرُ الرَّاجِى رَحْمَةَ رَبِّهِ الرَّحْمَانِيَّةِ ، صَالِحُ الْحُسَينِيُّ بْنُ مُحَمَّدِ بْنِ صَالِحِ الْجَعْفَرِيِّ الَّذِى إِلَى السَّيِّدِ جَعْفَرٍ الصَّادِقِ رَضِىَ اللهُ عَنْهُ نَسَبُهُ وَمُنْتَمَاهُ:

أَنَا تِلْمِيذُ ذِى المَعَارِفِ وَالإِرْشَادَاتِ إِلَى الطَّرِيقَةِ الأَحْمَدِيَّةِ وَالْخَتْمِيَّةِ ، السَّيِّدِ مُحَمَّدِ الشَّرِيفِ بْنِ السَّيِّدِ عَبْدِ العَالِي بْنِ السَّيِّدِ أَحْمَدَ بْنِ إِدْرِيسِ عَلَيْهِمْ رِضْوَانٌ مِنَ اللهِ بِعَدَدِ مَنْ أَخَذَ طَرِيقَهُمْ وَاسْتَعْذَبَ وِرْدَهُ وَتَلَاهُ ، وَتِلْمِيذُ الشَّيْخِ حَبِيبِ اللهِ الشَّنْقِيطِيِّ رَحِمَهُ اللهُ تَعَالَى فِى العُلُومِ وَالأَحَادِيثِ النَّبَوِيَّةِ ، وَالشَّيْخِ مُحَمَّدِ إِبْرَاهِيمَ المُحَدِّثِ وَالشَّيْخِ المُطِيعِيِّ وَالشَّيْخِ الدِّجْوِيِّ وَالشَّيْخِ الغُنَيمِيِّ وَغَيْرِهِمْ مِنْ اكَابِرِ عُلَمَاءِ الأَزْهَرِ الشَّرِيفِ عَلَيْهِمْ رَحْمَةٌ وَاسِعَةٌ تَدُومُ وَتَبْقَى مِنْ فَضْلِ اللهِ،

Sayyid Muḥammad Idrīs ﵁ has granted me *ijaza* with the highest, continuous chain in the Qur'ān, the books of ḥadith, and litanies of the path, from him to my master, Aḥmad b. Idrīs ﵁. And from him to our master and leader, the Messenger of Allāh ﷺ.

Allāh has favored me with the compilation of this honorable mawlid at the Islāmic University of al-Azhar. I have shortened and summarised some aspects of the biography of our master and leader, the Messenger of Allāh ﷺ.

In the beginning of composing it, I saw our master Jibrīl ﵇ in a clear vision. I greeted him and asked him for supplication, so he said to me, "Allāh will complete it." Thus, it was. Allāh ﷻ has completed this *mawlid* due to the blessing of the supplication of Jibrīl ﵇. Al-ḥamdu li-Llāh.

I am giving permission to every Muslim in all the Islāmic world, to recite this book every night of *Jumu'a* (Thursday night) and every Sunday night. I asked Allāh ﷻ to make the reading of this book a means for increasing wealth, safety, fulfilment of needs, and success to do such deeds that please Allāh.

O my brother in Allāh, it is necessary that you read this book with love, sincerity and correct intention. In shā' Allāh you will obtain what I asked for you and more, from the bounty of Allāh.

O Allāh send blessings, peace and abundance on our liege and master, Muḥammad, the best of creation, and on his family, in every glance and breath, as many times as all that is contained in the knowledge of Allāh.

وَقَدْ أَجَازَنِى السَّيِّدُ مُحَمَّدُ إِدْرِيسُ بِأَسَانِيدِهِ العَالِيَةِ المُتَّصِلَةِ السَّنِيَّةِ ، بِالقُرْآنِ العَظِيمِ، وَكُتُبِ الحَدِيثِ ، وَأَوْرَادِ الطَّرِيقِ مِنْهُ إِلَى سَيِّدِى أَحْمَدَ بْنِ إِدْرِيسَ رَضِىَ اللهُ عَنْهُ إِلَى سَيِّدِنَا وَمَوْلَانَا رَسُولِ اللهِ عَلَيْهِ صَلَوَاتُ اللهِ ،

قَدْ مَنَّ اللهُ عَلَىَّ بِتَأْلِيفِ هَذَا المَوْلِدِ الشَّرِيفِ بِالجَامِعِ الأَزْهَرِ ذِى العُلُومِ الأَزْهَرِيَّةِ ، اقْتَصَرْتُ فِيهِ مَعَ الإِيجَازِ عَلَى بَعْضِ سِيرَةِ سَيِّدِنَا وَمَوْلَانَا رَسُولِ اللهِ، وَفِى أَوَّلِ تَأْلِيفِهِ رَأَيْتُ فِى النَّوْمِ سَيِّدَنَا جِبْرِيلَ عَلَيْهِ السَّلَامُ رُؤْيَةً ظَاهِرَةً جَلِيَّةً ، فَسَلَّمْتُ عَلَيْهِ ، وَسَأَلْتُهُ الدُّعَاءَ ، فَقَالَ لِى : اللهُ يُتَمِّمْ ، فَتَمَّمَ اللهُ هَذَا المَوْلِدَ بِبَرَكَةِ دُعَائِهِ وَالحَمْدُ لِلهِ ، وَقَدْ أَجَزْتُ بِقِرَاءَتِهِ كُلَّ لَيْلَةِ جُمْعَةٍ وَلَيْلَةِ إِثْنَيْنِ كُلَّ مُسْلِمٍ فِى سَائِرِ الأَقْطَارِ الإِسْلَامِيَّةِ ، وَسَأَلْتُ اللهَ تَعَالَى أَنْ يَجْعَلَ قِرَاءَتَهُ سَبَباً فِى سَعَةِ الرِّزْقِ وَالعَافِيَةِ ، وَقَضَاءِ الحَوَائِجِ ، وَالتَّوْفِيقِ إِلَى مَا يُحِبُّهُ اللهُ تَعَالَى وَيَرْضَاهُ ، فَعَلَيْكَ يَا أَخَانَا فِى اللهِ تَعَالَى بِقِرَاءَتِهِ بِالمَحَبَّةِ وَالإِخْلَاصِ وَحُسْنِ النِّيَّةِ ، تَجِدْ إِنْ شَاءَ اللهُ تَعَالَى مَا دَعَوْتُ لَكَ بِهِ وَالمَزِيدَ مِنْ فَضْلِ اللهِ ،

﴿اللَّهُمَّ صَلِّ وَسَلِّمْ وَبَارِكْ عَلَى سَيِّدِنَا وَمَوْلَانَا مُحَمَّدٍ خَيْرِ البَرِيَّةِ،
وَعَلَى آلِهِ فِى كُلِّ لَمْحَةٍ وَنَفَسٍ عَدَدَ مَا وَسِعَهُ عِلْمُ اللهِ﴾

CHAPTER 2

The Best of Allāh's Creation ﷺ

Surely Muḥammad ﷺ is the most noble of Allāh's creation. The scholars of the past and present are unanimous that he ﷺ is the best of creation, the lofty [of them] and the lowly [of them]. He ﷺ said, "I am the leader of the progeny of Ādam and I am not boasting about it." Which means, 'I am not saying this to show pride, but to show the bounty of Allāh, which He has bestowed upon me.'

So, the first thing that Allāh ﷻ created was the light of his Muḥammadan essence, as it was reported by al-Ḥāfiẓ ʿAbd al-Razzāq al-Yamānī in his Musnad, narrated by Jābir b. ʿAbd Allāh.

Allāh ﷻ began his Prophethood in the realm of pre-eternity. As the Prophet ﷺ said, "I was a Prophet, while Ādam was still between the soul and body".

Abū ʿIsā al-Tirmidhī, also brought the above narration in his Sunan and affirmed it. Allāh ﷻ made the Prophet ﷺ the seal of the Prophets and the Messengers. No new prophet will come until the day those in their earthly graves are raised.

In pre-eternity, Allāh ﷻ took a covenant from all the prophets and messengers, that they believe in his Prophethood and that they will assist him; as has come and we have heard in the Majestic Qurʾān.

الفصل الثانى

أَنَّهُ صَلَّى اللهُ عَلَيْهِ وَسَلَّمَ أَفْضَلُ خَلْقِ اللهِ

قَدْ أَجْمَعَ العُلَمَاءُ سَلَفاً وَخَلَفاً عَلَى أَنَّهُ صَلَّى اللهُ عَلَيْهِ وَسَلَّمَ أَفْضَلُ المَخْلُوقَاتِ العُلْوِيَّةِ وَالسُّفْلِيَّةِ ، وَقَدْ قَالَ صَلَّى اللهُ عَلَيْهِ وَسَلَّمَ: أَنَا سَيِّدُ وَلَدِ آدَمَ وَلَا فَخْرَ ، أَىْ لَا يَقُولُ ذَلِكَ مُفْتَخِراً ، وَلَكِنْ تَحَدُّثاً بِمَا أَنْعَمَ اللهُ تَعَالَى بِهِ عَلَيْهِ وَأَوْلَاهُ ،

فَأَوَّلُ مَا خَلَقَ اللهُ تَعَالَى نُورَ ذَاتِهِ المُحَمَّدِيَّةِ ، كَمَا أَخْرَجَهُ الحَافِظُ عَبْدُ الرَّزَاقِ اليَمَنِيُّ فِى مُسْنَدِهِ عَنْ الأَنْصَارِىِّ جَابِرِ بْنِ عَبْدِ اللهِ ، وَافْتَتَحَ اللهُ تَعَالَى بِهِ صَلَّى اللهُ عَلَيْهِ وَسَلَّمَ النُّبُوَّةَ فِى العَوَالِمِ الأَزَلِيَّةِ ، كَمَا قَالَ صَلَّى اللهُ عَلَيْهِ وَسَلَّمَ: كُنْتُ نَبِياً وَآدَمُ بَيْنَ الرُّوحِ وَالجَسَدِ ، أَخْرَجَهُ أَبُو عِيسَى التِّرْمِذِىُّ فِى سُنَنِهِ وَارْتَضَاهُ، وَجَعَلَهُ اللهُ تَعَالَى خَاتَمَ النَّبِيِّينَ وَالمُرْسَلِينَ ، فَلَا نَبِىَّ بَعْدَهُ إِلَى يَوْمِ بَعْثِ مَنْ فِى القُبُورِ التُّرَابِيَّةِ ، وَقَدْ أَخَذَ اللهُ تَعَالَى المِيثَاقَ فِى الأَزَلِ عَلَى جَمِيعِ النَّبِيِّينَ وَالمُرْسَلِينَ عَلَيْهِمْ الصَّلَاةُ وَالسَّلَامُ بِأَنْ يُؤْمِنُوا بِرِسَالَتِهِ صَلَّى اللهُ عَلَيْهِ وَسَلَّمَ وَيَكُونُوا أَنْصَاراً لَهُ صَلَّى اللهُ عَلَيْهِ وَسَلَّمَ كَمَا جَاءَ فِى القُرْآنِ العَظِيمِ وَسَمِعْنَاهُ ،

The first of lights is his light ﷺ, from which all other Divine lights branched out, and from him spread forth secrets and burst forth lights. If the prophets were present in his time ﷺ, then most certainly they would have supported him, and they would have been under the banner of 'Lā ilāha illā Allāh, Muḥammadun Rasūl Allāh' ﷺ. Imām al-Nabhānī ؒ indicated this meaning when he said,

> Your light is the whole and the creation are parts thereof
> O Prophet, even the prophets are from your army.

Indeed, his honorable light appeared on the face of our father Ādam ؑ, by which his beauty and splendor dazzled the angels. If Iblīs had witnessed his light ﷺ, he would have been the first one to prostrate without any doubt or confusion.

My master, 'Alī Wafā ؒ said,

> If Shayṭān were to see the splendor of his light ﷺ
> in the face of Ādam, he would have been the first to make prostration.

O Allāh send blessings, peace and abundance on our liege and master, Muḥammad, the best of creation, and on his family, in every glance and breath, as many times as all that is contained in the knowledge of Allāh.

فَأَوَّلُ الأَنْوَارِ نُورُهُ صَلَّى اللهُ عَلَيْهِ وَسَلَّمَ الَّذِي مِنْهُ تَفَرَّعَتْ جَمِيعُ الأَنْوَارِ الإِلَهِيَّةِ، فَهُوَ صَلَّى اللهُ عَلَيْهِ وَسَلَّمَ مِنْهُ انْشَقَّتْ الأَسْرَارُ وَانْفَلَقَتْ الأَنْوَارُ، وَلَوْ حَضَرَ الأَنْبِيَاءُ زَمَانَهُ عَلَيْهِمْ الصَّلَاةُ وَالسَّلَامُ لَكَانُوا أَنْصَاراً لَهُ صَلَّى اللهُ عَلَيْهِ وَسَلَّمَ تَحْتَ رَايَةِ لَا إِلَهَ إِلَّا اللهُ مُحَمَّدٌ رَسُولُ اللهِ ، وَقَدْ أَشَارَ النَّبَهَانِيُّ إِلَى هَذَا المَعْنَى بِقَوْلِهِ :

نُـورُكَ الـكُلُّ وَالْـوَرَى أَجْـزَاءُ   يَـا نَبِيـاً مِـنْ جُنْـدِهِ الأَنْبِيـاَءُ

وَقَدْ ظَهَرَ نُورُهُ الشَّرِيفُ عَلَى وَجْهِ أَبِينَا آدَمَ عَلَيْهِ السَّلَامُ بِمَا أَبْهَرَ حُسْنُهُ وَضِيَاؤُهُ الجَمَاعَةَ المَلَكِيَّةَ ، وَلَوْ رَأَى إِبْلِيسُ نُورَهُ صَلَّى اللهُ عَلَيْهِ وَسَلَّمَ لَكَانَ أَوَّلَ مَنْ سَجَدَ بِلَا شَكٍّ وَلَا اشْتِبَاهٍ ،

قَالَ سَيِّدِى عَلِيٌّ وَفَا رَضِىَ اللهُ عَنْهُ :

لَـوْ أَبْـصَرَ الشَّـيْطَانُ طَلْعَـةَ نُـورِهِ   فِي وَجْـهِ آدَمَ كَانَ أَوَّلَ مَـنْ سَـجَدْ

﴿اللَّهُمَّ صَلِّ وَسَلِّمْ وَبَارِكْ عَلَى سَيِّدِنَا وَمَوْلَانَا مُحَمَّدٍ خَيْرِ البَرِيَّةِ،
وَعَلَى آلِهِ فِي كُلِّ لَمْحَةٍ وَنَفَسٍ عَدَدَ مَا وَسِعَهُ عِلْمُ اللهِ﴾

CHAPTER 3

That He is Nūr (Light) ﷺ

You should know that the Prophet ﷺ is a light unlike all other lights. Nay! His ﷺ light surpasses the lights of this world and the Hereafter! On the night of Miʿrāj, Jibrīl ﷺ said, "If I go even one step further, I will be burnt from the lights." So he ﷺ proceeded forth alone in those lights. How sublime and how strong is he ﷺ! Since the Prophet ﷺ is a light, stronger than that of Jibrīl, the veils were lifted for him and he saw his Lord ﷻ. And no one has seen Him other than him ﷺ.

Thus, he ﷺ is al-Sirāj al-Munīr (the Illuminating Lamp), that provides light to the hearts of the believers, be it human being or jinn, by his enduring sensory and spiritual lights.

The Prophet ﷺ is the one who truly hears. The one that heard the primordial speech of Allāh, without letters or words which are recited by the mouths.

The Prophet ﷺ is the one who truly sees. The one who beheld his Lord (without modality or limits), Glorified and Exalted is He from there being any other deity.

If the entire world, without exception, was in his place at the moment of theophanies, then without any doubt, all of it would have been reduced to mere dust particles. Glory be to the One Who made His Prophet ﷺ firm, gave him strength, assisted him and granted him [favors].

الفصل الثالث

وَأَنَّهُ صَلَّى اللهُ عَلَيْهِ وَسَلَّمَ نُورٌ

وَاعْلَمْ أَنَّهُ صَلَّى اللهُ عَلَيْهِ وَسَلَّمَ نُورٌ لا كَالأَنْوارِ، بَلْ يَفُوقُ جَمِيعَ الأَنْوَارِ الدُّنْيَوِيَّةِ وَالأُخْرَوِيَّةِ ، وَفِي لَيْلَةِ المِعْرَاجِ قَالَ جِبْرِيلُ عَلَيْهِ السَّلَامُ : لَوْ تَقَدَّمْتُ خَطْوَةً لَاحْتَرَقْتُ مِنَ الأَنْوَارِ فَتَقَدَّمَ صَلَّى اللهُ عَلَيْهِ وَسَلَّمَ وَحْدَهُ فِي تِلْكَ الأَنْوارِ، فَمَا أَجَلَّهُ وَمَا أَقْوَاهُ ،

وَلَمَّا كَانَ صَلَّى اللهُ عَلَيْهِ وَسَلَّمَ نُوراً أَقْوَى مِنَ الأَنْوَارِ الجِبْرَائِيلِيَّةِ ، كُشِفَ لَهُ الحِجَابُ ، فَرَأَى رَبَّهُ تَعَالَى ، وَمَا رَآهُ أَحَدٌ سِوَاهُ ، فَهُوَ صَلَّى اللهُ عَلَيْهِ وَسَلَّمَ السِّرَاجُ المُنِيرُ الَّذِي أَضَاءَ قُلُوبَ المُؤْمِنِينَ إِنْساً وَجِنًّا بِأَنْوَارِهِ البَاقِيَةِ الحِسِّيَّةِ وَالمَعْنَوِيَّةِ ، السَّمِيعُ الَّذِي سَمِعَ كَلَامَ رَبِّهِ القَدِيمَ بِلَا حَرْفٍ وَلَا صَوْتٍ وَلَا بِالْكَلِمَاتِ الَّتِي تُقْرَأُ بِالأَفْوَاهِ ، البَصِيرُ الَّذِي أَبْصَرَ رَبَّهُ بِلَا كَيْفٍ وَلَا انْحِصَارٍ ، سُبْحَانَهُ وَتَعَالَى مِنْ إِلَهٍ ، وَلَوْ كَانَتِ الدُّنْيَا بِحَذَافِيرِهَا فِي المَكَانِ الَّذِي كَانَ فِيهِ صَلَّى اللهُ عَلَيْهِ وَسَلَّمَ عِنْدَ التَّجَلِّي لَصَارَتْ كَالهَبَاءَاتِ الذَّرِيَّةِ ، فَسُبْحَانَ مَنْ ثَبَّتَ نَبِيَّهُ صَلَّى اللهُ عَلَيْهِ وَسَلَّمَ ، وَقَوَّاهُ وَأَيَّدَهُ وَأَعْطَاهُ ، وَأَمَّا أَنْوَارُهُ الحِسِّيَّةُ فَقَدْ

As for his physical light, many companions saw it and reported it through authentic sources.

His description ﷺ would overwhelm them, so sometimes they would say his light was like the sun, and sometimes they would say it was like the moon when it is in full beauty and splendor. They said that he ﷺ did not have a shadow due to the subtlety of his luminous essence ﷺ.

If it is asked: How is it possible that Muḥammad ﷺ became a man when he is light?

Answer: The angel Jibrīl ﷺ would come in the form of the companion Diḥyā [al-Kalbī] ؓ yet he is light, without doubt or confusion. Therefore, the One Who can make Jibrīl ﷺ, who is light, as a man in human form, is capable of making His beloved ﷺ, who is light, into a human being outwardly, so that we can speak with him and see him.

The sweat of the Prophet ﷺ was like musk in its fragrance and aroma, and like pearls in its color. Even though his body was like other bodies, yet it would emanate a strong and sweet fragrance. The companions would enhance their perfume with his ﷺ sweat and seek blessings by it, they would apply it on their children for the sake of blessings, as is mentioned by Imām al-Bukhārī.

It comes in the collections of ḥadith that the mother of the believers, Sayyida ʿĀʾisha ؓ, was sewing a garment at night; the needle fell from her hand and she could not find it, due to the darkness of the night. Just then the Prophet ﷺ entered, and immediately the place lit up (with his light) and she saw the needle. Upon this she composed a couplet praising the Messenger of Allāh ﷺ. The Prophet ﷺ became happy and kissed her forehead because of her praise of his complete enlightened being ﷺ. The above-mentioned narration is narrated in al-Khaṣāiṣ al-Kubrā by al-Ḥāfiẓ [Jalāl al-

رَآهَا كَثِيرٌ مِنَ الصَّحَابَةِ رَضِىَ اللهُ عَنْهُمْ بالرِّوَايَةِ الْجَلِيَّةِ ، وَكَانَ يَغْلِبُهُمْ وَصْفُهُ صَلَّى اللهُ عَلَيْهِ وَسَلَّمَ ، فَتَارَةً يَقُولُونَ كَالشَّمْسِ ، وَتَارَةً يَقُولُونَ ، كَالقَمَرِ عِنْدَ تَمَامِهِ فِى حُسْنِهِ وَمَرْآهُ ،وَقَالُوا : إِنَّهُ لَا ظِلَّ لَهُ لِلَطَافَةِ ذَاتِهِ النُّورَانِيَّةِ ،

فَإِنْ قِيلَ : كَيْفَ صَارَ صَلَّى اللهُ عَلَيْهِ وَسَلَّمَ رَجُلاً وَهُوَ نُورٌ ؟ يُجَابُ : بِأَنَّ جِبْرِيلَ كَانَ يَأْتِى فِى صُورَةِ الصَّحَابِّى دِحْيَةَ وَهُوَ نُورٌ بِلَا شَكٍّ وَلَا اشْتِبَاهٍ ، فَالَّذِى جَعَلَ جِبْرِيلَ عَلَيْهِ السَّلَامُ النُّورَ رَجُلاً فِى صُورَةٍ إِنْسَانِيَّةٍ ، قَادِرٌ عَلَى أَنْ يَجْعَلَ حَبِيبَهُ صَلَّى اللهُ عَلَيْهِ وَسَلَّمَ النُّورَ إِنْسَاناً ظَاهِراً كَىْ نُكَلِّمَهُ وَنَرَاهُ ، وَكَانَ عَرَقُهُ صَلَّى اللهُ عَلَيْهِ وَسَلَّمَ كَالْمِسْكِ طِيباً وَرِيحاً ، وَكَاللُّؤْلُؤِ لَوْناً ، وَلَوْ كَانَ جَسَدُهُ كَالأَجْسَادِ مَا ظَهَرَتْ تِلْكَ الرَّوَائِحُ الطَّيِّبَةُ الذَّكِيَّةُ ، وَكَانُوا يُصْلِحُونَ بِعَرَقِهِ ، طِيبَهُمْ وَيَتَبَرَّكُونَ بِهِ ، وَيَمْسَحُونَ بِهِ عَلَى أَطْفَالِهِمْ تَبَرُّكاً ، كَمَا أَخْرَجَ ذَلِكَ البُخَارِىُّ رَحِمَهُ اللهُ وَرَوَاهُ ،

قَدْ وَرَدَ فِى الْحَدِيثِ أَنَّ أُمَّ الْمُؤْمِنِينَ عَائِشَةَ رَضِىَ اللهُ عَنْهَا كَانَتْ تَخِيطُ ثَوْباً بِلَيْلٍ وَسَقَطَتِ الْإِبْرَةُ مِنْ يَدِهَا فَلَمْ تَهْتَدِ إِلَيْهَا لِظُلْمَةِ اللَّيلِ الظُّلْمَانِيَّةِ ، فَدَخَلَ النَّبِىُّ صَلَّى اللهُ عَلَيْهِ وَسَلَّمَ ، فَأَضَاءَ الْمَكَانُ وَرَأَتِ الإِبْرَةَ فَتَمَثَّلَتْ بِبَيْتٍ مِنَ الشِّعْرِ ثَنَاءً عَلَى رَسُولِ اللهِ ، فَسَرَّ النَّبِىَّ صَلَّى اللهُ عَلَيْهِ وَسَلَّمَ بِثِنَائِهَا وَقَبَّلَ رَأْسَهَا مِنْ أَجْلِ مَدْحِهَا لِذَاتِهِ الْمُكَمَّلَةِ النُّورَانِيَّةِ ، أَخْرَجَ هَذَا الْحَدِيثَ الْحَافِظُ السُّيُوطِىُّ

Dīn] al-Suyūṭī ﷺ, and he regarded this narration to have a good and acceptable chain.

Therefore, our brothers in Allāh, it is incumbent upon you to increase in the prayers on the Messenger of Allāh ﷺ. Especially the Ṣalāt al-ʿAẓīmiyya through which one may achieve what those who arrived have achieved, in witnessing his essence and his face ﷺ.

Once the Companions ﷺ were walking on a dark road, and a light accompanied them while they were walking together. When they separated, this light divided, and everyone had their own light until they reached their individual homes. That was from his light ﷺ![1]

The vision of the Prophet ﷺ has continued for those who follow al-Ṭarīqa al-Muḥammadiyya al-Aḥmadiyya. They have seen him ﷺ in a wakeful state just as our Shaykh, Sayyid Aḥmad b. Idrīs, Allāh be pleased with him and please him, has. This is narrated by Shaykh Sanūsī ﷺ in his books, manifest and clear. This bounty continues for those who travel his path, remember his awrād (litanies) and recite them.

O Allāh send blessings, peace and abundance on our liege and master, Muḥammad, the best of creation, and on his family, in every glance and breath, as many times as all that is contained in the knowledge of Allāh.

1 Bukhārī

رَحِمَهُ اللهُ فِي الْخَصَائِصِ الْكُبْرَى وَحَسَّنَ إِسْنَادَهُ وَارْتَضَاهُ ، فَعَلَيْكَ يَا أَخَانَا فِي اللهِ تَعَالَى بِالإِكْثَارِ مِنَ الصَّلَاةِ عَلَى رَسُولِ اللهِ صَلَّى اللهُ عَلَيْهِ وَسَلَّمَ ، وَلَا سِيَّمَا بِالصَّلَاةِ الْعَظِيمِيَّةِ ، تَنَلْ مَا نَالَهُ الْوَاصِلُونَ مِنْ مُشَاهَدَةِ ذَاتِهِ وَمُحَيَّاهُ ،

وَكَانَ الصَّحَابَةُ رَضِيَ اللهُ عَنْهُمْ إِذَا سَارُوا فِي طَرِيقٍ مُظْلِمٍ صَحِبَهُمُ النُّورُ يُضِيءُ لَهُمْ ، فَإِذَا تَفَرَّقُوا انْقَسَمَ النُّورُ وَصَارَ مَعَ كُلِّ وَاحِدٍ نُورٌ يُوَصِّلُهُ إِلَى دَارِهِ المَعْنِيَّةِ، وَذَلِكَ مِنْ نُورِهِ صَلَّى اللهُ عَلَيْهِ وَسَلَّمَ . أَخْرَجَ ذَلِكَ البُخَارِيُّ رَحِمَهُ اللهُ وَحَكَاهُ، وَلَا تَزَالُ رُؤْيَتُهُ صَلَّى اللهُ عَلَيْهِ وَسَلَّمَ يَقَظَةً مُسْتَمِرَّةً لِأَصْحَابِ الطَّرِيقَةِ الْمُحَمَّدِيَّةِ الْأَحْمَدِيَّةِ ، وَقَدْ رَأَوْهُ يَقَظَةً كَمَا حَصَلَ ذَلِكَ لِشَيْخِنَا السَّيِّدِ أَحْمَدَ بْنِ إِدْرِيسَ رَضِيَ اللهُ عَنْهُ وَأَرْضَاهُ ، وَقَدْ نَقَلَ ذَلِكَ السَّيِّدُ السَّنُوسِيُّ رَضِيَ اللهُ عَنْهُ فِي كُتُبِهِ الظَّاهِرَةِ الْجَلِيَّةِ ، وَقَدْ حَصَلَ لَهُ ذَلِكَ أَيْضًا ، وَلَا يَزَالُ مُسْتَمِرًّا ذَلِكَ الْفَضْلُ لِمَنْ سَلَكَ طَرِيقَهُ وَذَكَرَ وِرْدَهُ وَتَلَاهُ ،

﴿اللَّهُمَّ صَلِّ وَسَلِّمْ وَبَارِكْ عَلَى سَيِّدِنَا وَمَوْلَانَا مُحَمَّدٍ خَيْرِ الْبَرِيَّةِ،
وَعَلَى آلِهِ فِي كُلِّ لَمْحَةٍ وَنَفَسٍ عَدَدَ مَا وَسِعَهُ عِلْمُ اللهِ﴾

CHAPTER 4

His Spiritual Lights ﷺ

As for the spiritual lights of the Prophet ﷺ, they are countless and limitless. They are like oceans raging with spectacular waves. Since by him ﷺ, the hearts are illuminated and the egos are rectified. Allāh guided by him ﷺ, all those who were guided, to His guidance. How many are those that are raised from the graves of kufr (spiritual death), by his religion, as munificent champions!

Allāh ﷻ says in the Qur'ān: *As for the one who was dead, We revived him.* Meaning, the one who is dead by kufr (spiritually dead) is given life by responding to Allāh and His Messenger ﷺ. So good fortune to the one whom Allāh ﷻ has given success in that, and thus given him life!

Allāh ﷻ has honored, by him ﷺ, the best Umma (nation) brought out for mankind. He is the best of all creation and, by him ﷺ, his Umma is the leader of all previous nations. Allāh ﷻ says: *You are the best nation raised up for mankind.* This is due to the message of our master and leader, the Messenger of Allāh ﷺ. Allāh ﷻ has perpetuated the Magnificent Qur'ān with the continuation of the Muḥammadan sun, and it will continue preserved, benefiting, and guiding everyone that reads it and acts upon it. Allāh ﷻ has appointed the scholars as protectors of the luminous sunna. They remove from it such narrations that are not authentic

الفصل الرابع

فِى أَنْوَارِهِ الْمَعْنَوِيَّةِ صَلَّى اللهُ عَلَيْهِ وَسَلَّمَ

وَأَمَّا أَنْوَارُهُ الْمَعْنَوِيَّةُ فَلَا تُعَدُّ وَلَا تُحْصَى ، فَهِيَ بِحَارٌ مُتَلَاطِمَةُ الْأَمْوَاجِ الْجَوْهَرِيَّةِ، إِذْ بِهِ صَلَّى اللهُ عَلَيْهِ وَسَلَّمَ اسْتَنَارَتِ الْقُلُوبُ وَصَلَحَتِ النُّفُوسُ ، وَهَدَى اللهُ بِهِ لِهَدْيِهِ مَنْ هَدَاهُ ، فَكَمْ أَحْيَا مِنْ أَجْدَاثِ الْكُفْرِ بِدِينِهِ أَبْطَالاً ارْيَحِيَّةً ، قَالَ تَعَالَى: ﴿ أَوَ مَنْ كَانَ مَيْتاً فَأَحْيَيْنَاهُ ﴾ أَىْ مَيْتاً بِالْكُفْرِ فَأَحْيَاهُ بِالْاسْتِجَابَةِ لِلهِ تَعَالَى وَلِرَسُولِهِ صَلَّى اللهُ عَلَيْهِ وَسَلَّمَ فَيَا سَعْدَ مَنْ وَفَّقَهُ اللهُ لِذَلِكَ وَأَحْيَاهُ ، وَشَرَّفَ اللهُ بِهِ صَلَّى اللهُ عَلَيْهِ وَسَلَّمَ خَيْرَ أُمَّةٍ أُخْرِجَتْ لِلنَّاسِ وَهُوَ صَلَّى اللهُ عَلَيْهِ وَسَلَّمَ خَيْرُ الْخَلْقِ . وَأُمَّتُهُ سَادَتْ بِهِ عَلَى جَمِيعِ الْأُمَمِ الْقَبْلِيَّةِ، قَالَ تَعَالَى: ﴿كُنْتُمْ خَيْرَ أُمَّةٍ أُخْرِجَتْ لِلنَّاسِ﴾ ، وَذَلِكَ بِسَبَبِ رِسَالَةِ سَيِّدِنَا وَمَوْلَانَا رَسُولِ اللهِ ،

وَأَدَامَ اللهُ تَعَالَى الْقُرْآنَ الْعَظِيمَ بِدَوَامِ شَمْسِهِ الْمُحَمَّدِيَّةِ ، فَلَا يَزَالُ مَحْفُوظاً نَافِعاً هَادِياً لِكُلِّ مَنْ عَمِلَ بِهِ وَتَلَاهُ ، وَقَدْ قَيَّضَ اللهُ تَعَالَى لِلسُّنَّةِ الْغَرَّاءِ عُلَمَاءَ حَافَظُوا عَلَيْهَا ، وَأَبْعَدُوا عَنْهَا الْأَقْوَالَ الَّتِى لَيْسَتْ صَحِيحَةً مَرْضِيَّةً ، فَجَاءَتْ

or acceptable, hence the sunna has been handed down with authenticity and refinement, by trustworthy narrators. The one who travels is guided by its light through the darkness of the pitch-black nights. From the sunna, streams of knowledge and wisdom gush forth as from an ocean that has no end. Glory be to the One who has preserved His speech so that it becomes a guide to His *Sharīʿa* and *Kalima*: '*Lā ilāha illā Allāh*', the *kalima* of *tawḥīd* (pure monotheism). Furthermore, He preserved the sunna of His Prophet ﷺ so that it guides to his states ﷺ, and to the truthfulness of the statement 'Muḥammadun Rasūl Allāh' ﷺ.

O Allāh send blessings, peace and abundance on our liege and master, Muḥammad, the best of creation, and on his family, in every glance and breath, as many times as all that is contained in the knowledge of Allāh.

مُصحَّحَةً مُنقَّحَةً عَنِ الثِّقَاةِ مِنَ الرُّوَاةِ ، يَهْتَدِى السَّارِى بِنُورِهَا فِى الْحَوَالِكِ الحِنْدِسِيَّةِ ، وَتَتَفَجَّرُ مِنهَا يَنَابِيعُ الْعِلْمِ وَالْحِكْمَةِ مِنْ بَحْرٍ لَا يُدْرَكُ مَدَاهُ ،فَسُبْحَانَ مَنْ حَافَظَ عَلَى كَلَامِهِ لِيَكُونَ دَالاً عَلَى شَرِيعَتِهِ وَكَلِمَةِ « لَا إِلَهَ إِلَّا اللهُ » الْكَلِمَةِ التَّوْحِيدِيَّةِ ، وَحَافَظَ عَلَى سُنَّةِ نَبِيِّهِ صَلَّى اللهُ عَلَيْهِ وَسَلَّمَ ، لِتَكُونَ دَالَّةً عَلَى أَحْوَالِهِ صَلَّى اللهُ عَلَيْهِ وَسَلَّمَ ، وَصِدْقِ كَلِمَةِ «مُحَمَّدٌ رَسُولُ اللهِ» ،

﴿اللّٰهُمَّ صَلِّ وَسَلِّمْ وَبَارِكْ عَلَى سَيِّدِنَا وَمَوْلَانَا مُحَمَّدٍ خَيْرِ البَرِيَّةِ،
وَعَلَى آلِهِ فِي كُلِّ لَمْحَةٍ وَنَفَسٍ عَدَدَ مَا وَسِعَهُ عِلْمُ اللّٰهِ﴾

CHAPTER 5

Preservation of His Lineage ﷺ and the Transference of the Muḥammadan Light ﷺ

For the sake of the Prophet ﷺ, Allāh ﷻ has protected his lineage from fornication, shirk and idol worship, from the time of the Prophet Ādam, peace be upon him, to his grandfather, ʿAbd al-Muṭṭalib and his father, ʿAbd Allāh. The Muḥammadan light would transfer in their foreheads from Ādam, to his son, Shīth, to the forehead of our master Ibrāhīm ﷺ, the intimate friend (*al-Khalīl*), after his father, whose name was Tārikh, who was a believer without any doubt or confusion. The proof of his faith is in the statement of Allāh: *Our Sustainer, forgive me and my parents and the believers.*

In this verse, Ibrāhīm, peace be upon him, made a supplication for forgiveness for his parents; so if they were not believers, he would not have made supplication for them, and would not have included them with the believers. Therefore, take note of this wondrous, clear *masʾala* (legal ruling). As for that which Allāh mentions in His saying: '*When it became clear to him that he is an enemy of Allāh he became distant from him*'.

That was regarding his paternal uncle, Āzar, when Ibrāhīm presented Islām to him and he refused.

الفصل الخامس

فِى حِفْظِ نَسَبِهِ صَلَّى اللّٰهُ عَلَيْهِ وَسَلَّمَ ، وَتَنَقُّلِ النُّورِ الْمُحَمَّدِىِّ

وَمِنْ أَجْلِهِ صَلَّى اللّٰهُ عَلَيْهِ وَسَلَّمَ حَفِظَ اللّٰهُ تَعَالَى نَسَبَهُ مِنَ السِّفَاحِ وَالشِّرْكِ وَالْوَثَنِيَّةِ ، مِنْ سَيِّدِنَا آدَمَ عَلَيْهِ السَّلَامُ إِلَى جَدِّهِ صَلَّى اللّٰهُ عَلَيْهِ وَسَلَّمَ عَبْدِ الْمُطَّلِبِ وَأَبِيهِ عَبْدِ اللّٰهِ ، وَكَانَ النُّورُ الْمُحَمَّدِىُّ يَتَنَقَّلُ فِى جِبَاهِهِمْ مِنْ آدَمَ عَلَيْهِ السَّلَامُ إِلَى ابْنِهِ شِيثٍ عَلَيْهِ السَّلَامُ إِلَى جَبْهَةِ سَيِّدِنَا إِبْرَاهِيمَ الْخَلِيلِ عَلَيْهِ السَّلَامُ بَعْدَ وَالِدِهِ تَارِخَ الَّذِى كَانَ مُؤْمِناً بِلَا شَكٍّ وَلَا اشْتِبَاهٍ ، وَالدَّلِيلُ عَلَى إِيمَانِهِ قَوْلُ اللّٰهِ تَعَالَى : ﴿رَبَّنَا اغْفِرْ لِى وَلِوَالِدَىَّ وَلِلْمُؤْمِنِينَ﴾ ، فَقَدْ دَعَا عَلَيْهِ السَّلَامُ لِوَالِدَيْهِ بِالْمَغْفِرَةِ فَلَوْ لَمْ يَكُونَا مُؤْمِنَيْنِ مَا دَعَا لَهُمَا ، وَلَا عَطَفَ عَلَيْهِمَا الْمُؤْمِنِينَ . فَتَنَبَّهْ لِهَذِهِ الْمَسْأَلَةِ الْغَرِيبَةِ الْجَلِيَّةِ ، وَأَمَّا مَا حَكَاهُ اللّٰهُ تَعَالَى عَنْهُ بِقَوْلِهِ : ﴿فَلَمَّا تَبَيَّنَ لَهُ أَنَّهُ عَدُوٌّ لِلَّهِ تَبَرَّأَ مِنْهُ﴾ فَذَاكَ عَمُّهُ آزَرُ لَمَّا أَعْرَضَ عَنِ الإِسْلَامِ وَأَبَاهُ ، ثُمَّ لَا يَزَالُ النُّورُ الْمُحَمَّدِىُّ يَتَنَقَّلُ إِلَى أَنْ وَصَلَ إِلَى جَبْهَةِ عَبْدِ الْمُطَّلِبِ إِلَى ابْنِهِ عَبْدِ اللّٰهِ إِلَى السَّيِّدَةِ آمِنَةَ بِنْتِ وَهْبٍ كَمَا رَوَيْنَاهُ ،

وَقَدْ اخْتَارَ اللّٰهُ تَعَالَى لِنَبِيِّهِ صَلَّى اللّٰهُ عَلَيْهِ وَسَلَّمَ نَسَباً طَاهِراً مُطَهَّراً بِعَقْدِ

Thereafter the Muḥammadan light continued transferring until it reached the forehead of ʿAbd al-Muṭṭalib then to his son, ʿAbd Allāh and to Sayyida Āmina, the daughter of Wahb. Allāh has selected a pure and purified family lineage through matrimonial contract, free from the fornication of the days of *Jāhiliyya* (ignorance). This was an ennoblement due to the high worth and elevated status of the Prophet ﷺ with his Lord.

THE LINEAGE OF THE PROPHET

He is Sayyiduna Muḥammad ﷺ b. ʿAbd Allāh b. ʿAbd al-Muṭṭalib b. Hāshim, the mighty man; b. ʿAbd Manāf b. Quṣayy b. Kilāb, whose actual name was Ḥakīm; b. Murra b. Kaʿb b. Luʾayy b. Ghālib, the one who used to overpower his enemies with lion-like might; [b. Fihr], b. Mālik b. al-Naḍr, the one whose splendor of face was noticed by anyone who saw him; b. Kināna b. Khuzayma b. Mudrika b. Ilyās, who was the first person who slaughtered a camel as a sacrifice in the boundary of the Ḥaram; the Prophet ﷺ was heard, while he ﷺ was in his loins, remembering Allāh and saying to Allāh, "I am here at your service"; b. Muḍar b. Nizār b. Maʿadd b. ʿAdnān; just as it is mentioned in the prophetic narrations; and ʿAdnān's lineage goes up to our master Ibrāhīm, may Allāh's peace and blessings be upon our Prophet and upon him.

Most certainly this lineage has obtained the pinnacle of nobility, in as far as the human family lineage is concerned. It is the most virtuous of the creation in terms of status, and the most elevated and lofty in terms of reputation. ʿAbd al-Muṭṭalib was inspired to name the father of the Prophet ﷺ: ʿAbd Allāh. This is because ʿAbd Allāh's son ﷺ, would invite to the worship of Allāh alone, and would destroy shirk and idol worship. Likewise, Allāh has inspired Wahb

صَحِيحٍ خَالِصٍ مِنْ سِفَاحِ الْجَاهِلِيَّةِ ، إِكْرَاماً لِقَدْرِهِ العَالِى صَلَّى اللهُ عَلَيْهِ وَسَلَّمَ وَلِشَأْنِهِ الْمَرْفُوعِ عِنْدَ مَوْلَاهُ،

نَسَبُ النَّبِيِّ صَلَّى اللهُ عَلَيْهِ وَسَلَّمَ

فَهُوَ سَيِّدُنَا مُحَمَّدُ بْنُ عَبْدِ اللهِ بْنِ عَبْدِ الْمُطَّلِبِ بْنِ هَاشِمٍ ذِى الْيَدِ الْقَوِيَّةِ ، بْنِ عَبْدِ مَنَافِ بْنِ قُصَىِّ بْنِ كِلَابِ - واسْمُهُ حَكِيمٌ كَمَا رَوَيْنَاهُ - بْنِ مُرَّةَ بْنِ كَعْبِ بْنِ لُؤَىِّ بْنِ غَالِبٍ الَّذِى غَلَبَ أَعْدَاءَهُ بِقُوَّتِهِ الْأَسَدِيَّةِ ،[ابْنِ فِهْرِ] بْنِ مَالِكِ بْنِ النَّضْرِ الَّذِى عَلَى وَجْهِهِ نُضْرَةُ نُورٍ تَظْهَرُ لِكُلِّ مَنْ رَآهُ ، بْنِ كِنَانَةَ بْنِ خُزَيْمَةَ بْنِ مُدْرِكَةَ بْنِ إِلْيَاسَ وَهُوَ أَوَّلُ مَنْ نَحَرَ الْبُدْنَ هَدْياً بِالرِّحَابِ الْحَرَمِيَّةِ، وَسُمِعَ النَّبِيُّ صَلَّى اللهُ عَلَيْهِ وَسَلَّمَ وَهُوَ فِى صُلْبِهِ ذِكْرَ اللهِ تَعَالَى وَلَبَّاهُ ، بْنِ مُضَرَ بْنِ نِزَارِ بْنِ مَعَدِّ بْنِ عَدْنَانَ كَمَا وَرَدَ ذَلِكَ فِى الْأَحَادِيثِ النَّبَوِيَّةِ ، وَعَدْنَانُ يَنْتَهِى نَسَبُهُ إِلَى سَيِّدِنَا إِبْرَاهِيمَ عَلَى نَبِيِّنَا وَعَلَيْهِ صَلَوَاتُ اللهِ،

وَقَدْ حَازَ هَذَا النَّسَبُ ذِرْوَةَ الشَّرَفِ فِى الْأَنْسَابِ الْإِنْسَانِيَّةِ ، بِأَفْضَلِ الْخَلَائِقِ قَدْرًا وَأَرْفَعِهِمْ ذِكْراً وَأَعْلَاهُ ،

وَقَدْ أُلْهِمَ عَبْدُ الْمُطَّلِبِ أَنْ يُسَمِّىَ وَالِدَ النَّبِىِّ صَلَّى اللهُ عَلَيْهِ وَسَلَّمَ عَبْدَ اللهِ ، لِأَنَّ وَلَدَهُ سَيَدْعُو إِلَى عِبَادَةِ اللهِ وَحْدَهُ وَهَدْمِ الشِّرْكِ وَالْوَثَنِيَّةِ ، كَمَا أَلْهَمَ اللهُ وَهْباً

to name the mother of Prophet ﷺ: Āmina, because she will be the mother of the one who is the security of the creation and its guide ﷺ.

The lineage of Mustafa is like the pearl necklace,
    The Quraysh were honored with the dignity of Muḥammad ﷺ.

Allāh has protected his lineage with the best of protection,
    Everyone in it possesses glory and greatness.

A lineage from the intimate friend of the Generous Lord,
    To the Beloved who is the most distinguished and glorified.

O Allāh send blessings, peace and abundance on our liege and master, Muḥammad, the best of creation, and on his family, in every glance and breath, as many times as all that is contained in the knowledge of Allāh.

أَنْ يُسَمِّىَ أُمَّهُ صَلَّى اللهُ عَلَيْهِ وَسَلَّمَ آمِنَةَ لِأَنَّهَا سَتَكُونُ أُماً لِأَمْنِ الخَلْقِ وَهُدَاهُ،

نَسَبُ الْمُصْطَفَى كَعِقْدٍ مُضِيءٍ مِنْ كِرَامٍ تَشَرَّفُوا بِمُحَمَّدْ
حَفِظَ اللهُ عِقْدَهُ خَيْرَ حِفْظٍ كُلُّ مَنْ فِيهِ ذُو فَخَارٍ وَسُؤْدَدْ
نَسَبٌ مِنْ خَلِيلِ رَبٍّ كَرِيمٍ لِحَبِيبٍ مُشَرَّفٍ وَمُمَجَّدْ

﴿اللّٰهُمَّ صَلِّ وَسَلِّمْ وَبَارِكْ عَلَى سَيِّدِنَا وَمَوْلَانَا مُحَمَّدٍ خَيْرِ البَرِيَّةِ،
وَعَلَى آلِهِ فِي كُلِّ لَمْحَةٍ وَنَفَسٍ عَدَدَ مَا وَسِعَهُ عِلْمُ اللهِ﴾

CHAPTER 6

When His Mother Conceived Him ﷺ

When Āmina was pregnant with the Prophet ﷺ, she did not find any cravings nor any burden that a woman normally experiences during their pregnancy. This is because he is a light, so carrying him was no burden, as he ﷺ is unlike any other human being in his composition, both in the beginning of his affair and in the end.

It is narrated that during her pregnancy with him ﷺ, his mother witnessed astonishing things, whilst awake and in her dreams; for he ﷺ is the possessor of many spectacular miracles that no one other than him would receive.

The prophets and the messengers came in her dream, to give her pure and happy, glad tidings, because they too were delighted and glad with his coming ﷺ. This is because he is their *Imām*, who Allāh has selected for them, while being pleased with him ﷺ. She was ordered to name him 'Muḥammad', owing to the fact that he is the praiseworthy one with a life pleasing [to Allāh].

The Earth brought forth its greenness and drought disappeared, and the pastures became most pleasing to the shepherds, and an announcer proclaimed the nearness of his arrival ﷺ. The animals and beasts of the land and the sea became delighted. The angels rejoiced and were delighted with the approach of the time for the manifestation of the light of his beauty and countenance. The jinn

الفصل السادس

فِى حَمْلِ أُمِّهِ بِهِ صَلَّى اللّٰهُ عَلَيْهِ وَسَلَّمَ

وَلَمَّا حَمَلَتْ بِهِ أُمُّهُ صَلَّى اللّٰهُ عَلَيْهِ وَسَلَّمَ لَمْ تَجِدْ لِحَمْلِهِ وَحَماً ، وَلَا ثِقَلاً مِنَ الأُمُورِ العَادِيَّةِ ، لِأَنَّهُ نُورٌ لَا يَثْقُلُ حَمْلُهُ ، لَيْسَ كَالْخَلْقِ فِى تَكْوِينِهِ وَفِى أَوَّلِ أَمْرِهِ وَمُنْتَهَاهُ ،

وَقَدْ رَأَتْ أُمُّهُ صَلَّى اللّٰهُ عَلَيْهِ وَسَلَّمَ فِى أَثْنَاءِ حَمْلِهَا بِهِ صَلَّى اللّٰهُ عَلَيْهِ وَسَلَّمَ عَجَائِبَ فِى الْيَقَظَةِ وَالْمَنَامِ لَهَا مَحْكِيَّةً ، لِأَنَّهُ صَلَّى اللّٰهُ عَلَيْهِ وَسَلَّمَ صَاحِبُ الْمُعْجِزَاتِ البَاهِرَاتِ الَّتى مَا نَالَهَا أَحَدٌ سِوَاهُ ، وَبَشَّرَهَا الْأَنْبِيَاءُ وَالْمُرْسَلُونَ عَلَيْهِمُ الصَّلَاةُ وَالسَّلَامُ فِى مَنَامِهَا بِبِشَارَاتٍ طَيِّبَةٍ هَنِيَّةٍ ، لِأَنَّهُمْ فَرِحُونَ مُسْتَبْشِرُونَ بِهِ صَلَّى اللّٰهُ عَلَيْهِ وَسَلَّمَ ، لِأَنَّهُ إِمَامُهُمُ الَّذى اخْتَارَهُ اللّٰهُ تَعَالَى لَهُمْ وَارْتَضَاهُ ، وَأُمِرَتْ بِتَسْمِيَتِهِ مُحَمَّداً صَلَّى اللّٰهُ عَلَيْهِ وَسَلَّمَ ، لِأَنَّهُ مَحْمُودُ السِّيرَةِ الْمَرْضِيَّةِ ، وَاخْضَرَّتِ الْأَرْضُ ، وَذَهَبَ الْجَدْبُ ، وَطَابَ لِلرَّاعِى مَرْعَاهُ ، وَنَادَى مُنَادٍ بِقُرْبِ ظُهُورِهِ صَلَّى اللّٰهُ عَلَيْهِ وَسَلَّمَ . وَتَبَاشَرَتِ الْوُحُوشُ الْبَرِّيَّةُ وَالْبَحْرِيَّةُ، وَفَرِحَتِ الْمَلَائِكَةُ وَاسْتَبْشَرَتْ بِدُنُوِّ ظُهُورِ نُورِ جَمَالِهِ وَمُحَيَّاهُ ، وَهَتَفَتِ الْجِنُّ

hailed the drawing close of his birth ﷺ and manifestation of many tangible blessings.

And why shouldn't it be like this? For certainly it was the time for the Prophet of the Truth and Salvation to appear. The scholars of ḥadith have narrated [many] authentic ḥadith which the Umma has accepted and the reliable scholars have agreed on.

O Allāh send blessings, peace and abundance on our liege and master, Muḥammad, the best of creation, and on his family, in every glance and breath, as many times as all that is contained in the knowledge of Allāh.

بِقُرْبِ وِلَادَتِهِ صَلَّى اللهُ عَلَيْهِ وَسَلَّمَ ، وَظَهَرَتْ بَرَكَاتٌ حِسِّيَّةٌ ، وَكَيْفَ لَا يَكُونُ كَذَلِكَ وَقَدْ آنَ أَوَانُ ظُهُورِ نَبِيِّ الْحَقِّ وَالنَّجَاةِ ، وَقَدْ رَوَى ذَلِكَ الْمُحَدِّثُونَ فِي الْأَحَادِيثِ الصَّحِيحَةِ الْمَرْوِيَّةِ ، الَّتِي تَلَقَّتْهَا الْأُمَّةُ بِالْقَبُولِ ، وَارْتَضَاهَا الْأَئِمَّةُ الثِّقَاةُ ،

﴿اللّٰهُمَّ صَلِّ وَسَلِّمْ وَبَارِكْ عَلَى سَيِّدِنَا وَمَوْلَانَا مُحَمَّدٍ خَيْرِ البَرِيَّةِ،
وَعَلَى آلِهِ فِي كُلِّ لَمْحَةٍ وَنَفَسٍ عَدَدَ مَا وَسِعَهُ عِلْمُ اللهِ﴾

CHAPTER 7

Concerning His Birth ﷺ

After about two months into his mother's pregnancy with him ﷺ, his father passed away in the vicinity of Yathrib (Madīna). This was so that Allāh may take over the responsibility to nurture, direct, and guide him ﷺ.

Sayyidunā 'Alī was asked, Allāh be pleased with him and ennoble his countenance, "What was the wisdom in the death of the Prophet's parents ﷺ?" He said, "In order for Allāh alone to nurture him, a nurturing of compassion and mercy".

The Prophet ﷺ said, "My Lord taught me manners and has perfected my manners", and he ﷺ was the best of the people in manners, whether on a journey or at home.

The *ulama* deem it praiseworthy to stand at the mention of his birth ﷺ, in respect, honor, and happiness for the coming of the best of creation ﷺ. Success is for the one who loves and honors him, follows his sunna and supports him ﷺ.

Now comes the time for the illuminating moon of the era to light up the earth after nine lunar months, the one who will cover the universe with his light, until the end of time.

When Sayyida Āmina's water broke; Sayyida Āsiya, Sayyida Maryam ﷺ and the maidens of paradise arrived at her house, and she gave birth to him ﷺ, a shining light that filled the horizon with his light and splendor ﷺ.

الفصل السابع

فِي وِلَادَتِهِ صَلَّى اللهُ عَلَيْهِ وَسَلَّمَ

وَلَمَّا تَمَّ مِنْ حَمْلِ أُمِّهِ بِهِ صَلَّى اللهُ عَلَيْهِ وَسَلَّمَ شَهْرَانِ تُوُفِّيَ وَالِدُهُ بِالدِّيَارِ الْيَثْرِبِيَّةِ، لِيَتَوَلَّى اللهُ تَعَالَى تَرْبِيَتَهُ وَإِرْشَادَهُ وَهُدَاهُ ،

وَقَدْ سُئِلَ أَمِيرُ الْمُؤْمِنِينَ سَيِّدُنَا عَلِيٌّ رَضِيَ اللهُ عَنْهُ وَكَرَّمَ اللهُ وَجْهَهُ : مَا حِكْمَةُ مَوْتِ أَبَوَيِ النَّبِيِّ صَلَّى اللهُ عَلَيْهِ وَسَلَّمَ ؟ قَالَ: لِيَتَوَلَّى اللهُ تَرْبِيَتَهُ وَحْدَهُ تَرْبِيَةً رَحِيمَةً رَحْمَانِيَّةً ، وَقَالَ صَلَّى اللهُ عَلَيْهِ وَسَلَّمَ : «أَدَّبَنِي رَبِّي فَأَحْسَنَ تَأْدِيبِي» . فَكَانَ صَلَّى اللهُ عَلَيْهِ وَسَلَّمَ مِنْ أَحْسَنِ النَّاسِ أَدَباً فِي مُتَقَلَّبِهِ وَمَثْوَاهُ ، وَاسْتَحَبَّ الْعُلَمَاءُ الْقِيَامَ عِنْدَ ذِكْرِ وِلَادَتِهِ صَلَّى اللهُ عَلَيْهِ وَسَلَّمَ أَدَباً وَاحْتِرَامًا ، وَفَرَحاً بِقُدُومِ خَيْرِ الْبَرِيَّةِ ، فَيَا فَوْزَ مَنْ أَحَبَّهُ وَوَقَّرَهُ وَاتَّبَعَ سُنَّتَهُ وَوَالَاهُ ،

وَقَدْ آنَ لِقَمَرِ الزَّمَانِ أَنْ يَقْمُرَ الْأَرْضَ بَعْدَ تِسْعَةِ أَشْهُرٍ قَمَرِيَّةٍ ، وَيَعُمَّ الْكَوْنَ بِنُورِهِ إِلَى آخِرِ الزَّمَانِ وَمُنْتَهَاهُ ، فَأَجَاءَ آمِنَةَ الْمَخَاضُ وَقَدْ حَضَرَتْهَا آسِيَةُ وَمَرْيَمُ وَحُورٌ عَدْنِيَّةٌ ، فَوَضَعَتْهُ صَلَّى اللهُ عَلَيْهِ وَسَلَّمَ نُوراً سَاطِعاً مَلَأَ الْأُفُقَ ضَوْءُهُ وَسَنَاهُ ،

O Allāh bless Muḥammad,
O Allāh bless him and grant him peace

The lights of Ṭāhā shone,
like the sun in its mid-morning brightness

This world that we see,
is illuminated by Muḥammad

The birth of the guide, our Prophet,
gives delight to the grieved heart

Who can be more worthy to be our guide,
than the beloved, my master Muḥammad

He gave honor to the entire world
and came as an absolute truth and as an intercessor

He is obeyed and he obeys [the command of Allāh]
The chosen one of the Creator, Muḥammad

His face surpasses the full moon
The Master has increased him in happiness.

He has appeared in the universe as a Light,
before the [rest of the] creation of Allāh, [there is]
Muḥammad

The best of Allāh's creation is Ṭāhā,
like the sun in its mid-morning brightness

صَــلَّى اللهُ عَلَى مُحَمَّــدْ
صَــلَّى اللهُ عَلَيْــهِ وَسَــلَّمْ

أَشْرَقَــتْ أَنْــوَارُ طَــهَ
مِثْــلُ شَــمْسٍ فِى ضُحَاهَــا

هَــذِهِ الدُّنْيَــا نَرَاهَــا
فِى ضِيَــاءٍ مِــنْ مُحَمَّــدْ

مَــوْلِدُ الْهَــادِى نَبِينَــا
يُفْــرِحُ الْقَلْــبَ الْحَزِينَــا

مَــنْ بِــهِ حَقَّــا هُدِينَــا
الْحَبِيــبْ مَــوْلَاىْ مُحَمَّــدْ

شَرَّفَ الدُّنْيَــا جَمِيعَــا
وَأَتَى حَقَّــا شَــفِيعَا

وَمُطَــاعاً وَمُطِيعَــا
صَفْــوَةُ الْبَــارِى مُحَمَّــدْ

وَجْهُــهُ فَــاقَ الْبُــدُورَا
زَادَهُ الْمَــوْلَى سُرُوراً

قَــدْ بَــدَا فِى الْكَــوْنِ نُــورَا
قَبْــلَ خَلْــقِ اللهِ مُحَمَّــدْ

خَــيْرُ خَلْــقِ اللهِ طَــهَ
مِثْــلُ شَــمْسٍ فِى ضُحَاهَــا

هَــذِهِ الدُّنْيَــا نَرَاهَــا
فِى ضِيَــاءٍ مِــنْ مُحَمَّــدْ

نُــورُهُ عَــمَّ النَّــوَاحِى
لِظَــلَامِ الْكُفْــرِ مَاحِــى

فِى الصَّحَــارَى وَالبِطَــاحِ
أَشْرَقَــتْ أَنْــوَارْ مُحَمَّــدْ

فَظَهَرَ صَلَّى اللهُ عَلَيْهِ وَسَلَّمَ كَالشَّمْسِ الْمُضِيئَةِ الْبَهِيَّةِ ، نَظِيفاً دَهِيناً مَخْتُوناً، مَقْطُوعَ السُّرَّةِ ، وَقَدْ كُحِلَتْ بِإِثْمِدِ الْقُدْرَةِ الْإِلَهِيَّةِ عَيْنَاهُ ، وَاضِعاً يَدَيْهِ عَلَى الْأَرْضِ رَافِعاً رَأْسَهُ إِلَى السَّمَاءِ إِشَارَةً إِلَى العِزَّةِ وَالْكَرَامَةِ النَّبَوِيَّةِ ، لِأَنَّهُ كَانَ نَبِيًّا وَآدَمُ بَيْنَ الرُّوحِ وَالْجَسَدِ لَمْ يَظْهَرْ إِلَى الْوُجُودِ مَرْآهُ ، وَلَمَّا عَطَسَ حَمِدَ اللهَ

This world that we see,
is illuminated by Muḥammad

His light covers the horizons,
he is the eraser of the darkness of disbelief

In the deserts and the valleys,
shone the lights of Muḥammad.

He ﷺ appeared [in the world] like the bright, illuminating sun. He was born clean, his hair was naturally oiled, and he was circumcised. His umbilical cord was already cut, and his eyes were lined with the ithmid *kuḥl* of Divine might. He placed his hands on the ground, raising his head to the heavens, indicating the dignity and honor of prophethood, because he was a prophet while Ādam ﷺ was between soul and body and did not yet manifest into existence.

When he ﷺ sneezed, he praised Allāh for His eternal blessings and the angels replied to him by saying, "May Allāh have mercy upon you, O one who has honored the world by his coming and appearance."

O Allāh send blessings, peace and abundance on our liege and master, Muḥammad, the best of creation, and on his family, in every glance and breath, as many times as all that is contained in the knowledge of Allāh.

تَعَالَى عَلَى نِعَمِهِ السَّرْمَدِيَّةِ ، وَشَمَّتَتْهُ الْأَمْلَاكُ بِقَوْلِهَا : رَحِمَكَ اللهُ يَا مَنْ تَشَرَّفَتِ الدُّنْيَا بِقُدُومِهِ وَرُؤْيَاهُ ،

﴿اللّٰهُمَّ صَلِّ وَسَلِّمْ وَبَارِكْ عَلَى سَيِّدِنَا وَمَوْلَانَا مُحَمَّدٍ خَيْرِ الْبَرِيَّةِ، وَعَلَى آلِهِ فِي كُلِّ لَمْحَةٍ وَنَفَسٍ عَدَدَ مَا وَسِعَهُ عِلْمُ اللهِ﴾

CHAPTER 8

His Muʿjiza (miracles) on the Night He Was Born ﷺ

The night in which the Prophet ﷺ was born, the lights spread to such an extent that the Persian palaces were clearly seen, and the stars bowed down. The house was illuminated to the extent that his splendor lit up the Ḥaram. The palace of Kisrā shook from the Muḥammadan gravity and the fires of Persia were extinguished from every temple. The water of Lake Sāwa disappeared and the Samāwa valley flooded, and water overflowed from it.

O Allāh send blessings, peace and abundance on our liege and master, Muḥammad, the best of creation, and on his family, in every glance and breath, as many times as all that is contained in the knowledge of Allāh.

الفصل الثامن

مُعْجِزَاتُهُ صَلَّى اللّٰهُ عَلَيْهِ وَسَلَّمَ لَيْلَةَ الْوِلَادَةِ

وَفِي لَيْلَةِ مَوْلِدِهِ صَلَّى اللّٰهُ عَلَيْهِ وَسَلَّمَ انْتَشَرَتِ الْأَنْوَارُ حَتَّى تَرَاءَتِ الْقُصُورُ الكِسْرَوِيَّةُ ، وَتَدَلَّتِ النُّجُومُ وَاسْتَنَارَ الْبَيْتُ حَتَّى أَضَاءَ الْحَرَمَ سَنَاهُ ، وَتَصَدَّعَ إِيوَانُ كِسْرَى لِلْهَيْبَةِ الْمُحَمَّدِيَّةِ ، وَأُخْمِدَتْ نَارُ فَارِسٍ بِالدِّيَارِ الْفَارِسِيَّةِ ، وَغَاضَتْ بُحَيْرَةُ سَاوَةَ وَفَاضَ وَادِي سَمَاوَةَ وَتَفَجَّرَتْ مِنْهُ الْمِيَاهُ ،

﴿اللّٰهُمَّ صَلِّ وَسَلِّمْ وَبَارِكْ عَلَى سَيِّدِنَا وَمَوْلَانَا مُحَمَّدٍ خَيْرِ البَرِيَّةِ،
وَعَلَى آلِهِ فِي كُلِّ لَمْحَةٍ وَنَفَسٍ عَدَدَ مَا وَسِعَهُ عِلْمُ اللّٰهِ﴾

CHAPTER 9

His Nursing ﷺ

Ḥalīma al-Saʿdiyya ؓ nursed the Prophet ﷺ, so Allāh changed her difficulty to ease, and blessed her provision and made it flourish. She was delighted with him ﷺ and she directed her heart's love to him. She was fortunate to have him, and she accepted Islām and was buried in al-Baqīʿ [in Madīna]. May Allāh's mercy be upon her and the occupants of al-Baqīʿ.

He ﷺ would grow in a day how a child would normally grow in a month. He stood on his own at three months, and was walking at five months, and at nine months his strength reached completion.

When he turned three or four, two angels came to him and split open his chest without the aid of a knife. They washed his heart and removed a black lump of flesh, in order to cut off the influence of Shayṭān in the time of his youth. He ﷺ grew perfect and complete during his childhood and similarly in maturity, and was called '*al-Amīn*' (the Trustworthy one) due to his trustworthiness, truthfulness, good character and piety ﷺ.

O Allāh send blessings, peace and abundance on our liege and master, Muḥammad, the best of creation, and on his family, in every glance and breath, as many times as all that is contained in the knowledge of Allāh.

الفصل التاسع

فى رضاعه صَلَّى اللهُ عَلَيْهِ وَسَلَّمَ

وَأَرْضَعَتْهُ صَلَّى اللهُ عَلَيْهِ وَسَلَّمَ حَلِيمَةُ السَّعْدِيَّةُ ، فَأَبْدَلَ اللهُ عُسْرَهَا يُسْراً وَبَارَكَ لَهَا فِي رِزْقِهَا وَنَمَّاهُ ، وَفَرِحَتْ بِهِ وَوَجَّهَتْ إِلَيْهِ الْمَحَبَّةَ الْقَلْبِيَّةَ ، فَسَعِدَتْ بِهِ وَأَسْلَمَتْ وَدُفِنَتْ بِالْبَقِيعِ فَعَلَيْهَا وَعَلَى أَهْلِ الْبَقِيعِ رَحْمَةُ اللهِ ،

وَكَانَ صَلَّى اللهُ عَلَيْهِ وَسَلَّمَ يَنْمُو فِي الْيَوْمِ نُمُوَّ الطِّفْلِ فِي شَهْرٍ ثَلَاثِينَ يَوْماً زَمَانِيَّةً، فَقَامَ عَلَى قَدَمَيْهِ فِي ثَلَاثٍ وَمَشَى فِي خَمْسٍ هِلَالِيَّةٍ وَفِي تِسْعٍ تَكَامَلَتْ لَهُ صَلَّى اللهُ عَلَيْهِ وَسَلَّمَ جَمِيعُ قُوَاهُ ، وَجَاءَهُ مَلَكَانِ وَشَقَّا صَدْرَهُ وَذَلِكَ بَعْدَ ثَلَاثِ سِنِينَ أَوْ أَرْبَعٍ مِنْ غَيْرِ مُدْيَةٍ حَدِيدِيَّةٍ ، وَغَسَلَاهُ وَأَخْرَجَا مِنْهُ مُضْغَةً سَوْدَاءَ لِيُقْطَعَ حَظُّ الشَّيْطَانِ عَنْهُ فِي حِينِ صِبَاهُ ، فَنَشَأَ صَلَّى اللهُ عَلَيْهِ وَسَلَّمَ كَامِلًا مُكَمَّلًا فِي عَهْدِ الطُّفُولَةِ الْأَوَّلِيَّةِ ، وَكَذَلِكَ فِي عَهْدِ الرُّجُولَةِ وَدُعِيَ بِالْأَمِينِ لِأَمَانَتِهِ وَصِدْقِهِ وَحُسْنِ أَدَبِهِ وَتَقْوَاهُ ،

﴿اللَّهُمَّ صَلِّ وَسَلِّمْ وَبَارِكْ عَلَى سَيِّدِنَا وَمَوْلَانَا مُحَمَّدٍ خَيْرِ الْبَرِيَّةِ،
وَعَلَى آلِهِ فِي كُلِّ لَمْحَةٍ وَنَفَسٍ عَدَدَ مَا وَسِعَهُ عِلْمُ اللهِ﴾

CHAPTER 10

The Expansion of His Noble Chest ﷺ

From the special traits of the Prophet ﷺ, which none of the Prophets of mankind have preceded him in, is the splitting of his noble chest four times. This indicates the fact that Allāh had taken charge of his ﷺ affairs from the beginning until the end.

The first time his chest was split open was when he was in the lands of the Banī Sa'd, whilst with Ḥalīma al-Sa'diyya ﷺ. Since he would soon face the period of childhood, Allāh ﷻ washed his noble heart, so that he will be innocent of and protected from Shayṭān and his misleading troops.

Then his chest was opened a second time when he attained maturity, as he ﷺ was entering into the period of manhood. On this occasion, his heart was filled with perfection, firmness, majesty and light; the splendor of which brightened his surroundings.

Even in the days of ignorance, the Prophet ﷺ was a light and Allāh inspired him with behaviour that was in accordance with the Muḥammadan Shari'a. Such that he loved goodness and he would detest evil, and would seclude himself for the intimate discourse with his Lord. Many a time he would seclude himself in the cave of Ḥirā in a state of witnessing, supplication and intimate discourse.

Then Allāh ﷻ opened his chest ﷺ for the third time, when he completed his fortieth year. This time it was to prepare him for

الفصل العاشر

فِى شَرْحِ صَدْرِهِ الشَّرِيفِ صَلَّى اللهُ عَلَيْهِ وَسَلَّمَ

وَمِنْ خَصَائِصِهِ صَلَّى اللهُ عَلَيْهِ وَسَلَّمَ الَّتِى لَمْ يَسْبِقْهُ بِهَا أَحَدٌ مِنْ أَنْبِيَاءِ الْأُمَمِ الْإِنْسَانِيَّةِ ، شَرْحُ صَدْرِهِ الشَّرِيفِ أَرْبَعَ مَرَّاتٍ وَذَلِكَ يَدُلُّ عَلَى أَنَّ اللهَ تَعَالَى تَوَلَّى أَمْرَهُ فِى بَدْئِهِ وَمُنْتَهَاهُ ، وَكَانَ أَوَّلُ مَا شُرِحَ صَدْرُهُ صَلَّى اللهُ عَلَيْهِ وَسَلَّمَ بِأَرْضِ بَنِى سَعْدٍ عِنْدَ حَلِيمَةَ السَّعْدِيَّةِ ، لِأَنَّهُ صَلَّى اللهُ عَلَيْهِ وَسَلَّمَ سَيَسْتَقْبِلُ عَهْدَ الطُّفُولَةِ فَغَسَلَ اللهُ تَعَالَى قَلْبَهُ الشَّرِيفَ لِيَكُونَ صَلَّى اللهُ عَلَيْهِ وَسَلَّمَ مَعْصُوماً مِنَ الشَّيْطَانِ وَجُنُودِهِ الْغُوَاةِ ، ثُمَّ شُرِحَ صَدْرُهُ صَلَّى اللهُ عَلَيْهِ وَسَلَّمَ مَرَّةً ثَانِيَةً عِنْدَ الْبُلُوغِ لِأَنَّهُ صَلَّى اللهُ عَلَيْهِ وَسَلَّمَ سَيَلْقَى عَهْدَ الرُّجُولَةِ الْآدَمِيَّةِ، فَمُلِئَ قَلْبُهُ صَلَّى اللهُ عَلَيْهِ وَسَلَّمَ كَمَالاً وَثَبَاتاً وَجَلَالاً وَنُورًا يُضِيءُ حَوْلَهُ سَنَاهُ، فَكَانَ صَلَّى اللهُ عَلَيْهِ وَسَلَّمَ فِى الْجَاهِلِيَّةِ نُورًا أَلْهَمَهُ اللهُ تَعَالَى السُّلُوكَ بِمَا يُوَافِقُ الشَّرِيعَةَ الْمُحَمَّدِيَّةَ ، يُحِبُّ الْخَيْرَ وَيَكْرَهُ الشَّرَّ وَيَخْتَلِى بِمُنَاجَاةِ رَبِّهِ وَكَمْ قَدْ اخْتَلَى بِغَارِ حِرَاءَ فِى شُهُودٍ وَدُعَاءٍ وَمُنَاجَاةٍ ، ثُمَّ شَرَحَ اللهُ تَعَالَى صَدْرَهُ صَلَّى اللهُ عَلَيْهِ وَسَلَّمَ لِلْمَرَّةِ الثَّالِثَةِ بَعْدَ تَمَامِ أَرْبَعِينَ سَنَةً حَوْلِيَّةً ، وَذَلِكَ لِلتَّأَهُّبِ لِنُزُولِ الْوَحْيِ الَّذِى

the Revelation, for which Allāh ﷻ had chosen him from amongst His creation and made it for him exclusively. This was so that he would become firm before [the revelation of] the Magnificent Qur᾿ān. The book, that if it were to be revealed on a mountain, it would have crumbled out of awe of its immensity. The Prophet ﷺ had more firmness than the mighty mountains and was stronger than the noble angels, because his Lord ﷻ made him firm and strengthened him ﷺ.

Then Allāh ﷻ opened his chest for the fourth time on the night of *Isrā᾿* and Mi῾rāj. Allāh filled his heart with knowledge, wisdom, faith and certainty, to prepare him to behold his Lord and Master.

And Allāh ﷻ revealed to him this verse, reminding him ﷺ of this evident favor: *'Have We not expanded your breast'*

Allāh ﷻ elevated his mention ﷺ such that Allāh is not mentioned except that our Master Muḥammad, the Messenger of Allāh ﷺ, is mentioned with Him.

O Allāh send blessings, peace and abundance on our liege and master, Muḥammad, the best of creation, and on his family, in every glance and breath, as many times as all that is contained in the knowledge of Allāh.

اخْتَارَهُ اللهُ تَعَالَى لَهُ مِنْ بَيْنِ خَلْقِهِ وَاصْطَفَاهُ ، لِيَكُونَ صَلَّى اللهُ عَلَيْهِ وَسَلَّمَ ثَابِتاً أَمَامَ الْقُرْآنِ الْعَظِيمِ الَّذِى لَوْ نَزَلَ عَلَى جَبَلٍ لَتَدَكْدَكَ مِنْ هَيْبَتِهِ الْجَلَالِيَّةِ ،

فَكَانَ صَلَّى اللهُ عَلَيْهِ وَسَلَّمَ أَثْبَتَ مِنَ الْجِبَالِ الرَّاسِيَاتِ وَأَقْوَى مِنَ الْمَلَائِكَةِ الْكِرَامِ بِمَا ثَبَّتَهُ بِهِ رَبُّهُ سُبْحَانَهُ وَقَوَّاهُ ، ثُمَّ شَرَحَ اللهُ تَعَالَى صَدْرَهُ صَلَّى اللهُ عَلَيْهِ وَسَلَّمَ فِى الْمَرَّةِ الرَّابِعَةِ فِى لَيْلَةِ الْإِسْرَاءِ وَالْعُرُوجِ إِلَى السَّمَوَاتِ الْعُلْوِيَّةِ، وَمَلَأَ اللهُ تَعَالَى قَلْبَهُ صَلَّى اللهُ عَلَيْهِ وَسَلَّمَ عُلُومًا وَحِكَمًا وَإِيمَانًا وَيَقِينًا كَىْ يَسْتَعِدَّ لِمُشَاهَدَةِ رَبِّهِ وَمَوْلَاهُ ، وَقَدْ أَنْزَلَ اللهُ تَعَالَى عَلَيْهِ قَوْلَهُ : ﴿أَلَمْ نَشْرَحْ لَكَ صَدْرَكَ﴾ مُمْتَناً عَلَيْهِ صَلَّى اللهُ عَلَيْهِ وَسَلَّمَ بِهَذِهِ النِّعَمِ الْجَلِيَّةِ ، وَرَفَعَ اللهُ تَعَالَى ذِكْرَهُ صَلَّى اللهُ عَلَيْهِ وَسَلَّمَ ، فَمَا ذُكِرَ اللهُ تَعَالَى إِلَّا وَذُكِرَ مَعَهُ سَيِّدُنَا مُحَمَّدٌ صَلَّى اللهُ عَلَيْهِ وَسَلَّمَ رَسُولُ اللهِ ،

﴿اللَّهُمَّ صَلِّ وَسَلِّمْ وَبَارِكْ عَلَى سَيِّدِنَا وَمَوْلَانَا مُحَمَّدٍ خَيْرِ الْبَرِيَّةِ،
وَعَلَى آلِهِ فِى كُلِّ لَمْحَةٍ وَنَفَسٍ عَدَدَ مَا وَسِعَهُ عِلْمُ اللهِ﴾

CHAPTER 11

Earning a Livelihood and Marriage

The Prophet ﷺ would eat from the work of his own hands and would not depend on anyone from the men of Quraysh. When he ﷺ reached the age of twenty-five, he travelled to Syria for trade on behalf of Khadīja (رضي الله عنها), who had the good fortune of serving him ﷺ and gained his pleasure. She sent Maysara to assist him ﷺ in business related matters. He (Maysara) saw the angels shading him ﷺ which he did not see happening for anyone else. Maysara informed Khadīja (رضي الله عنها) of this incident and he praised the best of creation ﷺ before her. She said to him, "Indeed, I too have noticed that when he arrived, and I realized that he is a truthful and godly man." The business was profitable; Allāh had put many blessings in it due to the blessing of Prophethood.

Khadīja (رضي الله عنها) then proposed to him for marriage after realizing that he was a man of virtue and status. He ﷺ presented this proposal to his uncles and they accepted and welcomed her, due to her good noble character. His uncle, Abū Ṭālib, took charge of the marriage contract and delivered the marriage sermon wherein he praised the Prophet ﷺ and declared him to be pure.

She lived with him, a wonderful and pleasant life. All his male and female children were from her, with the exception of his son Ibrāhīm (عليه السلام), whose mother (Mārīya (رضي الله عنها)) was from Egypt and was

الفصل الحادى عشر

فِى كَسْبِهِ وَزَوَاجِهِ صَلَّى اللهُ عَلَيْهِ وَسَلَّمَ

وَكَانَ صَلَّى اللهُ عَلَيْهِ وَسَلَّمَ يَأْكُلُ مِنْ كَسْبِ يَدِهِ وَلَمْ يَكُنْ مُعْتَمِدًا عَلَى أَحَدٍ مِنَ الْفِئَةِ الْقُرَشِيَّةِ ، وَلَمَّا بَلَغَ صَلَّى اللهُ عَلَيْهِ وَسَلَّمَ خَمْسَةً وَعِشْرِينَ سَنَةً سَافَرَ إِلَى الشَّامِ فِى تِجَارَةٍ لِخَدِيجَةَ رَضِىَ اللهُ عَنْهَا الَّتِى سَعِدَتْ بِخِدْمَتِهِ صَلَّى اللهُ عَلَيْهِ وَسَلَّمَ وَرِضَاهُ ، وَأَرْسَلَتْ مَعَهُ صَلَّى اللهُ عَلَيْهِ وَسَلَّمَ مَيْسَرَةَ لِخِدْمَتِهِ صَلَّى اللهُ عَلَيْهِ وَسَلَّمَ فِى الْأُمُورِ التِّجَارِيَّةِ ، فَرَأَى الْمَلَائِكَةَ تُظَلِّلُهُ صَلَّى اللهُ عَلَيْهِ وَسَلَّمَ ، وَلَمْ يَرَ ذَلِكَ لِأَحَدٍ سِوَاهُ ، فَأَخْبَرَ خَدِيجَةَ بِذَلِكَ وَأَثْنَى لَهَا عَلَى خَيْرِ الْبَرِيَّةِ، فَقَالَتْ لَهُ: إِنَّنِى قَدْ رَأَيْتُ ذَلِكَ عِنْدَ قُدُومِهِ صَلَّى اللهُ عَلَيْهِ وَسَلَّمَ فَعَلِمْتُ أَنَّهُ الصَّادِقُ الْأَوَّاهُ ، وَقَدْ رَبِحَتِ التِّجَارَةُ وَبَارَكَ اللهُ فِيهَا بِالْبَرَكَةِ النَّبَوِيَّةِ ،

فَخَطَبَتْهُ صَلَّى اللهُ عَلَيْهِ وَسَلَّمَ لِنَفْسِهَا بَعْدَ أَنْ عَلِمَتْ أَنَّهُ ذُو فَضْلٍ وَجَاهٍ ، فَعَرَضَ ذَلِكَ صَلَّى اللهُ عَلَيْهِ وَسَلَّمَ عَلَى أَعْمَامِهِ فَقَبِلُوا ذَلِكَ وَرَحَّبُوا بِهَا مِنْ أَجْلِ أَخْلَاقِهَا الطَّيِّبَةِ السَّنِيَّةِ، وَتَوَلَّى الْعَقْدَ عَمُّهُ أَبُو طَالِبٍ ، وَخَطَبَ خُطْبَةَ الزَّوَاجِ وَأَثْنَى عَلَيْهِ صَلَّى اللهُ عَلَيْهِ وَسَلَّمَ وَزَكَّاهُ ،

given to him ﷺ as a gift (by the Egyptian ruler). Allāh bestowed the mother of the believers, Sayyida Khadīja, with many great and special traits. For example, He honored her with Sayyida Fāṭima, the Resplendent, from whom came the progeny of the beloved of Allāh and His chosen one ﷺ.

Allāh accepted the supplication of his Prophet ﷺ when he asked Him saying: *"O Lord, I beseech You to grant me a coolness of my eyes that will not be cut off."*

Verily, that is al-Zahrā' (the Resplendent) and her pure, prophetic offspring. May Allāh perpetuate her progeny until the Day of Judgement, guiding people to the path of Allāh.

O Allāh send blessings, peace and abundance on our liege and master, Muḥammad, the best of creation, and on his family, in every glance and breath, as many times as all that is contained in the knowledge of Allāh.

فَعَاشَتْ مَعَهُ صَلَّى اللهُ عَلَيْهِ وَسَلَّمَ عِيشَةً طَيِّبَةً هَنِيَّةً ، وَجَمِيعُ أَوْلَادِهِ وَبَنَاتِهِ صَلَّى اللهُ عَلَيْهِ وَسَلَّمَ مِنْهَا إِلَّا إِبْرَاهِيمَ عَلَيْهِ السَّلَامُ فَإِنَّ أُمَّهُ مِنْ مِصْرَ وَقَدْ جَاءَتْ لِلنَّبِيِّ صَلَّى اللهُ عَلَيْهِ وَسَلَّمَ هَدِيَّةً مُهْدَاةً ، وَقَدْ اخْتَصَّ اللهُ تَعَالَى أُمَّ الْمُؤْمِنِينَ السَّيِّدَةَ خَدِيجَةَ رَضِيَ اللهُ عَنْهَا بِأَعْظَمِ خُصُوصِيَّةٍ ، فَأَكْرَمَهَا بِالسَّيِّدَةِ فَاطِمَةَ الزَّهْرَاءِ رَضِيَ اللهُ عَنْهَا الَّتِي مِنْهَا ذُرِّيَّةُ حَبِيبِ اللهِ تَعَالَى وَمُصْطَفَاهُ ، وَقَدْ أَجَابَ اللهِ تَعَالَى دَعْوَةَ نَبِيِّهِ صَلَّى اللهُ عَلَيْهِ وَسَلَّمَ حَيْثُ قَالَ : « اللَّهُمَّ إِنِّي أَسْأَلُكَ قُرَّةَ عَيْنٍ لَا تَنْقَطِعُ » أَلَا وَهِيَ الزَّهْرَاءُ وَعِتْرَتُهَا الطَّاهِرَةُ النَّبَوِيَّةُ ، أَدَامَ اللهُ ذُرِّيَّتَهَا إِلَى يَوْمِ الْقِيَامَةِ هَادِينَ إِلَى صِرَاطِ اللهِ ،

﴿اللَّهُمَّ صَلِّ وَسَلِّمْ وَبَارِكْ عَلَى سَيِّدِنَا وَمَوْلَانَا مُحَمَّدٍ خَيْرِ الْبَرِيَّةِ،
وَعَلَى آلِهِ فِي كُلِّ لَمْحَةٍ وَنَفَسٍ عَدَدَ مَا وَسِعَهُ عِلْمُ اللهِ﴾

CHAPTER 12

Placing of the Black Stone in the Sacred House

When the Prophet ﷺ reached the age of thirty-five, the Quraysh intended to restore the *Ka'ba*, as it was damaged due to flooding. They differed as to who would place the black stone in its place. The disagreement between the various tribes intensified and the trial became great. They said, "The first to enter this door will judge between us." Then suddenly they were in the presence of the best of creation ﷺ. When they saw him, they were delighted and happy, and said, "This is the truthful, trustworthy one, all of us are pleased with him." He ﷺ spread out his shawl and placed the black stone upon it, and then ordered every tribe to take each of its corners; so they did that with pleasure. When they carried it, the Prophet ﷺ took it with his noble hand and placed the stone in its place. And so, Allāh had protected the stone from being touched by the hands of the disbelievers and honored it by the Prophet ﷺ, who raised it to its place with his own hands ﷺ. He ﷺ said, "The black stone is the right hand of Allāh on the earth." It is for this reason that he ﷺ kissed it, as has been reported by 'Umar ﷺ. This became an acted upon sunna and the person is rewarded for kissing it, and Allāh loves him and is pleased with him.

الفصل الثانى عشر

فِى وَضعِ الْحَجَرِ الْأَسْوَدِ فِى الْبَيْتِ الْحَرَامِ

وَلَمَّا بَلَغَ صَلَّى اللهُ عَلَيْهِ وَسَلَّمَ مِنَ الْعُمُرِ خَمْسَةً وَثَلَاثِينَ سَنَةً أَرَادُوا تَجْدِيدَ بِنَاءِ الكَعْبَةِ لِمَا أَصَابَهَا مِنَ السُّيُولِ الْمَطَرِيَّةِ ، وَاخْتَلَفُوا فِيمَنْ يَضَعُ الْحَجَرَ الْأَسْوَدَ وَاشْتَدَّ الْخِلَافُ بَيْنَ الْقَبَائِلِ وَعَظُمَتْ بَلْوَاهُ ، فَقَالُوا : أَوَّلُ دَاخِلٍ مِنْ هَذَا الْبَابِ يَحْكُمُ بَيْنَنَا فَإِذَا هُمْ بِخَيْرِ الْبَرِيَّةِ ، فَلَمَّا رَأَوْهُ صَلَّى اللهُ عَلَيْهِ وَسَلَّمَ اسْتَبْشَرُوا وَفَرِحُوا وَقَالُوا هَذَا الصَّادِقُ الْأَمِينُ وَكُلُّنَا يَرْضَاهُ ، فَبَسَطَ صَلَّى اللهُ عَلَيْهِ وَسَلَّمَ رِدَاءَهُ وَوَضَعَ الْحَجَرَ الْأَسْوَدَ عَلَيْهِ وَأَمَرَ كُلَّ قَبِيلَةٍ أَنْ تَأْخُذَ بِطَرَفٍ مِنْ أَطْرَافِهِ فَفَعَلُوا ذَلِكَ بِنَفْسٍ رَضِيَّةٍ ، فَلَمَّا حَمَلُوهُ أَخَذَهُ النَّبِيُّ صَلَّى اللهُ عَلَيْهِ وَسَلَّمَ بِيَدِهِ الشَّرِيفَةِ وَوَضَعَهُ فِى مَبْنَاهُ ،

وَقَدْ حَفِظَ اللهُ الْحَجَرَ مِنْ لَمْسِ أَيَادِى الْفِئَاتِ الْكُفْرِيَّةِ ، وَشَرَّفَهُ بِالنَّبِيِّ صَلَّى اللهُ عَلَيْهِ وَسَلَّمَ حَيْثُ رَفَعَتْهُ إِلَى مَكَانِهِ يَدَاهُ ، وَقَالَ صَلَّى اللهُ عَلَيْهِ وَسَلَّمَ: «الْحَجَرُ الْأَسْوَدُ يَمِينُ اللهِ فِى الْأَرْضِ» وَمِنْ أَجْلِ ذَلِكَ قَبَّلَهُ صَلَّى اللهُ عَلَيْهِ وَسَلَّمَ، كَمَا فِى الرِّوَايَةِ الْعُمَرِيَّةِ ، وَصَارَتْ سُنَّةً مُتَّبَعَةً يُثَابُ فَاعِلُهَا وَيُحِبُّهُ اللهُ وَيَرْضَاهُ ،

O Allāh send blessings, peace and abundance on our liege and master, Muḥammad, the best of creation, and on his family, in every glance and breath, as many times as all that is contained in the knowledge of Allāh.

﴿اللّٰهُمَّ صَلِّ وَسَلِّمْ وَبَارِكْ عَلَى سَيِّدِنَا وَمَوْلَانَا مُحَمَّدٍ خَيْرِ الْبَرِيَّةِ،
وَعَلَى آلِهِ فِي كُلِّ لَمْحَةٍ وَنَفَسٍ عَدَدَ مَا وَسِعَهُ عِلْمُ اللهِ﴾

CHAPTER 13

Beginning of Revelation

The Prophet ﷺ would see in his dreams what would occur in the future of his military expeditions. Never did he see a dream except that it would manifest like the break of dawn, without any doubt or confusion. At this time, seclusion and being distant from the creation was made beloved to him ﷺ. He ﷺ would go to worship in the cave of Ḥirāʾ by the inspiration that he received from Allāh, which directed him and singled him out for [Allāh] Himself. This was to prepare him to receive the revelation of the Qurʾānic verses. And when the revelation came to him, his Master sent him to the creation [to invite them]. The Angel came to him in the cave of Ḥirāʾ with the opening verses of *Sūra al-ʿAlaq*, and that was an announcement of the Muḥammadan Prophethood.

Then he returned to Khadīja ﷺ and said, "Most certainly, today I fear for myself" Then he informed her of what he had heard and seen. She remarked, "By Allāh, He will never debase you, O possessor of virtue, goodness and concern; who confers benefit to the entire creation. Indeed, you join family ties, you entertain the guest, you carry the burden of the down-trodden and you assist a person in need until he gets what he asked for."

Then the Angel came to him on another occasion, this time in his house, and brought the opening verses of *Sūra al-Muddaththir*.

الفصل الثالث عشر

فِى بِدْءِ الْوَحْيِ

وَكَانَ صَلَّى اللهُ عَلَيْهِ وَسَلَّمَ يَرَى فِى مَنَامِهِ مَا سَيَحْصُلُ فِى مُسْتَقْبَلِهِ مِنَ الْحَالَاتِ الْجِهَادِيَّةِ ، فَمَا رَأَى رُؤْيَا إِلَّا وَجَاءَتْ مِثْلَ فَلَقِ الصُّبْحِ بِلَا شَكٍّ وَلَا اشْتِبَاهٍ ، ثُمَّ حُبِّبَ إِلَيْهِ صَلَّى اللهُ عَلَيْهِ وَسَلَّمَ الْخَلَاءُ وَالْبُعْدُ عَنِ الْخَلَائِقِ بِالْكُلِّيَّةِ ، فَكَانَ صَلَّى اللهُ عَلَيْهِ وَسَلَّمَ يَتَعَبَّدُ فِى غَارِ حِرَاءَ بِإِلْهَامٍ مِنَ اللهِ تَعَالَى الَّذِى وَجَّهَهُ إِلَيْهِ وَاجْتَبَاهُ ، وَذَلِكَ اسْتِعْدَادًا لِتَلَقِّى الْوَحْيِ بِالْآيَاتِ الْقُرْآنِيَّةِ ، إِلَى أَنْ جَاءَهُ الْوَحْىُ وَأَرْسَلَهُ إِلَى الْخَلِيقَةِ مَوْلَاهُ ، فَجَاءَهُ الْمَلَكُ بِغَارِ حِرَاءَ بِأَوَّلِ سُورَةِ الْعَلَقِ فَكَانَ ذَلِكَ إِخْبَاراً بِالنُّبُوَّةِ الْمُحَمَّدِيَّةِ ،

فَرَجَعَ إِلَى خَدِيجَةَ رَضِىَ اللهُ عَنْهَا ، وَقَالَ صَلَّى اللهُ عَلَيْهِ وَسَلَّمَ : لَقَدْ خَشِيتُ الْيَوْمَ عَلَى نَفْسِى وَأَخْبَرَهَا بِمَا سَمِعَهُ وَرَآهُ ، فَقَالَتْ : وَاللهِ لَا يُخْزِيكَ اللهُ أَبَدًا يَا ذَا الْفَضْلِ وَالْخَيْرَاتِ وَالْإِعَانَاتِ الَّتِى إِلَى الْخَلَائِقِ مَسْدِيَّةٌ ، إِنَّكَ لَتَصِلُ الرَّحِمَ ، وَتَقْرِى الضَّيْفَ ، وَتَحْمِلُ الْكَلَّ ، وَتُعِينُ ذَا الْحَاجَةِ حَتَّى يَصِلَ إِلَى مُنَاهُ ، ثُمَّ جَاءَهُ صَلَّى اللهُ عَلَيْهِ وَسَلَّمَ مَرَّةً أُخْرَى فِى بَيْتِهِ بِأَوَّلِ سُورَةِ الْمُدَّثِّرِ ، فَكَانَ ذَلِكَ بَدْءَ

Thus, it was the beginning of '*al-Risalā al-Muṣṭafawiyya*' (The Chosen Messengership).

Now the Prophet ﷺ stood as an inviter, a spokesman, and a reminder. And his speech has been reported by many narrators.

He stayed in Makka for thirteen years, calling the creation towards the true religion. Whoever Allāh wanted salvation and guidance for, believed in him ﷺ. The first of those who believed in him ﷺ were Sayyiduna Abū Bakr al-Ṣiddīq ؓ, Sayyiduna 'Alī ؓ, the mother of the believers Sayyida Khadīja ؓ, and Sayyiduna Bilāl b. Rabāḥ ؓ, who used to call the *adhān* for the five daily compulsory prayers. Thereafter, the following people accepted Islām: Sayyiduna Uthmān ؓ, Sayyiduna Sa'd ؓ, Sayyiduna Sa'īd ؓ, Sayyiduna Ṭalḥa ؓ and Sayyiduna 'Abd al-Raḥmān b. 'Awf ؓ, whom the Prophet ﷺ gave the title '*Tājir al-Raḥmān*' (the businessman of the Most Beneficent), due to his generosity and affluence. Then Sayyiduna Zubayr b. 'Awwām ؓ accepted Islām, whose mother was Sayyida Ṣafiyya ؓ, the paternal aunt of the Prophet ﷺ. Then, Abū Ḥafṣ, Sayyiduna 'Umar ؓ accepted Islām. The day he accepted Islām, the Muslims prayed at the Ka'ba for the first time.

Then many of those who would become the *Muhājirūn* (migrants) accepted Islām. They are those who left their homes and their belongings for the propagation of Islām. Allāh gave them the title of 'Muhājirūn' because of their migration to Ṭayba (Madīna) with the one whom Allāh has raised and exalted his mention ﷺ.

O Allāh send blessings, peace and abundance on our liege and master, Muḥammad, the best of creation, and on his family, in every glance and breath, as many times as all that is contained in the knowledge of Allāh.

الرِّسَالَةِ الْمُصْطَفَوِيَّةِ ، فَقَامَ صَلَّى اللهُ عَلَيْهِ وَسَلَّمَ دَاعِياً وَخَطِيبًا وَمُذَكِّراً بِخُطْبَتِهِ الَّتِي رَوَاهَا عَنْهُ الرُّوَاهُ ، فَمَكَثَ بِمَكَّةَ ثَلَاثَ عَشْرَةَ سَنَةً يَدْعُو الْخَلَائِقَ إِلَى الْمِلَّةِ الْحَنِيفِيَّةِ ، فَآمَنَ بِهِ صَلَّى اللهُ عَلَيْهِ وَسَلَّمَ مَنْ أَرَادَ اللهُ تَعَالَى سَعَادَتَهُ وَهُدَاهُ ،

فَأَوَّلُ مَنْ آمَنَ بِهِ صَلَّى اللهُ عَلَيْهِ وَسَلَّمَ سَيِّدُنَا أَبُو بَكْرٍ الصِّدِّيقُ وَسَيِّدُنَا عَلِيٌّ ، وَأُمُّ الْمُؤْمِنِينَ السَّيِّدَةُ خَدِيجَةُ وَبِلَالُ بْنُ رَبَاحٍ الَّذِى كَانَ يُؤَذِّنُ لِلصَّلَوَاتِ الْفَرْضِيَّةِ ، ثُمَّ أَسْلَمَ سَيِّدُنَا عُثْمَانُ ، وَسَيِّدُنَا سَعْدٌ ، وَسَيِّدُنَا سَعِيدٌ ، وَسَيِّدُنَا طَلْحَةُ ، وَسَيِّدُنَا عَبْدُ الرَّحْمٰنِ بْنُ عَوْفٍ الَّذِى لَقَّبَهُ النَّبِيُّ صَلَّى اللهُ عَلَيْهِ وَسَلَّمَ بِتَاجِرِ الرَّحْمٰنِ لِكَرَمِهِ وَغِنَاهُ ، ثُمَّ أَسْلَمَ سَيِّدُنَا الزُّبَيْرُ بْنُ الْعَوَّامِ الَّذِى أُمُّهُ عَمَّةُ النَّبِيِّ صَلَّى اللهُ عَلَيْهِ وَسَلَّمَ وَهِيَ السَّيِّدَةُ صَفِيَّةُ ، ثُمَّ أَسْلَمَ أَبُو حَفْصٍ سَيِّدُنَا عُمَرُ الَّذِى يَوْمَ إِسْلَامِهِ صَلَّوْا عِنْدَ الْكَعْبَةِ أَوَّلَ صَلَاةٍ ، ثُمَّ أَسْلَمَ كَثِيرٌ مِنَ الْمُهَاجِرِينَ الَّذِينَ هَجَرُوا دِيَارَهُمْ وَتَرَكُوا أَمْلَاكَهُمْ مِنْ أَجْلِ نَشْرِ الدَّعْوَةِ الْإِسْلَامِيَّةِ ، وَسَمَّاهُمُ اللهُ تَعَالَى الْمُهَاجِرِينَ لِهِجْرَتِهِمْ إِلَى طَيْبَةَ مَعَ مَنْ رَفَعَ اللهُ ذِكْرَهُ وَأَعْلَاهُ ،

﴿اللّٰهُمَّ صَلِّ وَسَلِّمْ وَبَارِكْ عَلَى سَيِّدِنَا وَمَوْلَانَا مُحَمَّدٍ خَيْرِ الْبَرِيَّةِ،
وَعَلَى آلِهِ فِي كُلِّ لَمْحَةٍ وَنَفَسٍ عَدَدَ مَا وَسِعَهُ عِلْمُ اللهِ﴾

CHAPTER 14

Isrā᾽ and Mi'raaj

While the Prophet ﷺ was resting near the Kaʿba in Makka, Sayyiduna Jibrīl ﷺ, Sayyiduna Mikā᾽īl ﷺ and another angel came to him suddenly and they carried him to the well of *Zamzam*. After that, Jibrīl ﷺ, approached and took hold of him ﷺ, and split his noble chest ﷺ from below the throat till his illuminated navel. Then he removed his noble heart and washed it with *Zamzam* water, and filled it with wisdom, knowledge, and faith, to prepare him to behold his Creator and Master ﷻ.

Then the *Burāq* was brought forward for him ﷺ, with a saddle and rein. It was one of the animals from the highest levels of Paradise. The Prophet ﷺ then mounted the *Burāq*, while Sayyiduna Jibrīl ﷺ held the saddle and Sayyiduna Mikā᾽īl ﷺ held the rein. That was his point of departure and journey from Masjid al-Ḥarām to Masjid al-Aqṣā, which is in Shām. All of this took place with body and soul in the state of wakefulness, and this is by consensus of the gnostic scholars from the verifying narrators, of the early community and the latter.

And most certainly, Allāh ﷻ unveiled to him ﷺ astonishing hidden realities while on his way to Bayt al-Maqdis, which none before him ﷺ were shown. This was all due to his lofty status with his Creator and Master ﷻ.

الفصل الرابع عشر

فِي الْإِسْرَاءِ وَالْمِعْرَاجِ

بَيْنَمَا النَّبِيُّ صَلَّى اللهُ عَلَيْهِ وَسَلَّمَ مُضْطَجِعًا عِنْدَ الْحِجْرِ بِالْأَرَاضِي الْمَكِّيَّةِ ، إِذْ جَاءَهُ سَيِّدُنَا جِبْرِيلُ وَسَيِّدُنَا مِيكَائِيلُ وَمَعَهُمَا مَلَكٌ آخَرُ فَحَمَلُوهُ صَلَّى اللهُ عَلَيْهِ وَسَلَّمَ إِلَى زَمْزَمَ وَبَعْدَ ذَلِكَ جِبْرِيلُ عَلَيْهِ السَّلَامُ أَقْبَلَ عَلَيْهِ صَلَّى اللهُ عَلَيْهِ وَسَلَّمَ وَتَوَلَّاهُ ، وَشَقَّ صَدْرَهُ الشَّرِيفَ مِنْ ثَغْرَةِ نَحْرِهِ إِلَى سُرَّتِهِ النُّورَانِيَّةِ ، وَأَخْرَجَ قَلْبَهُ الشَّرِيفَ وَغَسَلَهُ بِمَاءِ زَمْزَمَ وَمَلَأَهُ حِكَماً وَعُلُوماً وَإِيمَاناً لِيَتَهَيَّأَ لِمُشَاهَدَةِ خَالِقِهِ وَمَوْلَاهُ ،

ثُمَّ جِئَ لَهُ صَلَّى اللهُ عَلَيْهِ وَسَلَّمَ بِالْبُرَاقِ مُسْرَجاً مُلْجَماً وَهُوَ دَابَّةٌ مِنْ دَوَابِّ الْجَنَّةِ الْعُلْوِيَّةِ ، فَرَكِبَهُ صَلَّى اللهُ عَلَيْهِ وَسَلَّمَ وَأَخَذَ سَيِّدُنَا جِبْرِيلُ بِرِكَابِهِ وَسَيِّدُنَا مِيكَائِيلُ بِزِمَامِ الْبُرَاقِ وَذَلِكَ هُوَ سَفَرُهُ وَمَسْرَاهُ ، مِنَ الْمَسْجِدِ الْحَرَامِ إِلَى الْمَسْجِدِ الْأَقْصَى بِالْبِلَادِ الشَّامِيَّةِ ، وَذَلِكَ بِجَسَدِهِ وَرُوحِهِ فِي حَالِ الْيَقَظَةِ بِإِجْمَاعِ الْعُلَمَاءِ الْعَارِفِينَ سَلَفاً وَخَلَفاً مِنَ الْمُحَقِّقِينَ الرُّوَاةِ ، وَقَدْ كَشَفَ اللهُ تَعَالَى لَهُ فِي طَرِيقِ سَيْرِهِ إِلَى بَيْتِ الْمَقْدِسِ عَنْ آيَاتٍ بَدِيعَةٍ غَيْبِيَّةٍ ، مَا نَالَهَا أَحَدٌ قَبْلَهُ صَلَّى اللهُ

Allāh ﷻ gathered all the prophets and messengers عليهم السلام, in body and in soul, and clothed; as Allāh protected their bodies from being consumed by the Earth.

Sayyiduna Jibrīl عليه السلام, gave the adhān and then advanced the Prophet ﷺ to the front, so he became their imām. This is because he ﷺ is the most virtuous of them, and he is their imām in prayer and outside it, in terms of Lordly virtues. He has the Grand Intercession when the other messengers عليهم السلام will excuse themselves. He ﷺ will be the first to intercede on that day when distress will reach its pinnacle.

Then different varieties of drink were brought in front of him and he ﷺ chose milk. Upon this, Jibrīl عليه السلام, said, "You have chosen the drink of fiṭra."

After that, he was brought the Mi'raj, which is a ladder made of gold and silver steps. He ﷺ ascended to the first Heaven. At this point Jibrīl عليه السلام, asked for the door to be opened. It was said from behind the door, "Who is with you?" He replied, "It is Muḥammad ﷺ". The guard, upon receiving the reply, opened the door and welcomed the Prophet ﷺ and greeted him. Upon reaching the first heaven, he saw Sayyiduna Adam عليه السلام, in his natural form. In the second heaven, he found Sayyiduna Yaḥyā عليه السلام and Sayyiduna 'Isā عليه السلام. In the third heaven, he found Sayyiduna Yūsuf عليه السلام, the possessor of magnificent beauties, whom Allāh gave half of all beauty. In the fourth heaven, he found Sayyiduna Idrīs عليه السلام, whom Allāh raised and granted a high status. In the fifth heaven, he found Sayyiduna Hārūn عليه السلام, who was the beloved of the Israelites. In the sixth heaven, he found Sayyiduna Mūsā b. 'Imrān عليه السلام, who encouraged the Prophet ﷺ to return to Allāh ﷻ to reduce the number of units of prayer.

In the seventh heaven, he found Sayyiduna Ibrahim عليه السلام, reclining next to al-Bayt al-Ma'mūr (the Ka'ba of the angels) in the company

عَلَيْهِ وَسَلَّمَ وَذَلِكَ لِعُلُوِّ قَدْرِهِ عِنْدَ خَالِقِهِ وَمَوْلَاهُ ،

وَجَمَعَ اللهُ تَعَالَى لَهُ صَلَّى اللهُ عَلَيْهِ وَسَلَّمَ النَّبِيِّينَ وَالْمُرْسَلِينَ عَلَيْهِمُ الصَّلَاةُ وَالسَّلَامُ بِأَجْسَامِهِمْ وَأَرْوَاحِهِمْ وَمَلَابِسِهِمْ وَذَلِكَ لِأَنَّ اللهَ حَفِظَ أَجْسَادَهُمْ مِنْ أَنْ تَأْكُلَهَا الطَّبَقَاتُ الْأَرْضِيَّةُ ، فَأَذَّنَ جِبْرِيلُ عَلَيْهِ السَّلَامُ لِلصَّلَاةِ ثُمَّ قَدَّمَ النَّبِيَّ صَلَّى اللهُ عَلَيْهِ وَسَلَّمَ فَصَارَ إِمَامَهُمْ فِي الصَّلَاةِ ، لِأَنَّهُ صَلَّى اللهُ عَلَيْهِ وَسَلَّمَ أَفْضَلُهُمْ وَإِمَامُهُمْ فَهُوَ صَلَّى اللهُ عَلَيْهِ وَسَلَّمَ إِمَامُهُمْ فِي الصَّلَاةِ وَغَيْرِهَا مِنَ الْفَضَائِلِ الرَّبَّانِيَّةِ ، وَلَهُ الشَّفَاعَةُ الْكُبْرَى عِنْدَ اعْتِذَارِ الرُّسُلِ عَلَيْهِمُ الصَّلَاةُ وَالسَّلَامُ عَنْهَا فَهُوَ صَلَّى اللهُ عَلَيْهِ وَسَلَّمَ أَوَّلُ الشُّفَعَاءِ يَوْمَ أَنْ يَبْلُغَ الْكَرْبُ مُنْتَهَاهُ ، ثُمَّ أُتِيَ صَلَّى اللهُ عَلَيْهِ وَسَلَّمَ بِأَشْرِبَةٍ فَاخْتَارَ اللَّبَنَ فَقَالَ جِبْرِيلُ عَلَيْهِ السَّلَامُ : قَدْ اخْتَرْتَ الشَّرْبَةَ الْفِطْرِيَّةَ ،

ثُمَّ جِئَ لَهُ صَلَّى اللهُ عَلَيْهِ وَسَلَّمَ بِالْمِعْرَاجِ وَهُوَ سُلَّمٌ مِرْقَاةٌ مِنَ الْفِضَّةِ وَمِرْقَاةٌ مِنَ الْمَعَادِنِ الذَّهَبِيَّةِ ، فَرَقَى بِهِ صَلَّى اللهُ عَلَيْهِ وَسَلَّمَ إِلَى السَّمَاءِ الدُّنْيَا حَيْثُ اسْتَفْتَحَ جِبْرِيلُ عَلَيْهِ السَّلَامُ فَقِيلَ لَهُ: وَمَنْ مَعَكَ؟ فَقَالَ : مُحَمَّدٌ صَلَّى اللهُ عَلَيْهِ وَسَلَّمَ فَفَتَحَ الْخَازِنُ الْبَابَ وَرَحَّبَ بِالنَّبِيِّ صَلَّى اللهُ عَلَيْهِ وَسَلَّمَ وَحَيَّاهُ ، وَلَمَّا وَصَلَ إِلَى السَّمَاءِ الْأُولَى رَأَى فِيهَا سَيِّدَنَا آدَمَ عَلَيْهِ السَّلَامُ عَلَى صُورَتِهِ الْأَوَّلِيَّةِ، وَفِي السَّمَاءِ الثَّانِيَةِ وَجَدَ سَيِّدَنَا يَحْيَى وَسَيِّدُنَا عِيسَى عَلَيْهِمَا صَلَوَاتُ اللهِ ، وَفِي

of the illuminated angels. Sayyiduna Ibrahim ﷺ said to him ﷺ, "O Muḥammad, convey my salām to your Nation." Upon our Prophet and Sayyiduna Ibrahim be the best blessing and most perfect peace, whose fragrance is spread throughout the universe. Then he ﷺ saw the *Sidrat al-Muntahā* (Lote Tree of the furthest boundary), the point where Divine commands end. Thereafter, he ﷺ saw Paradise, with all that is in it, and Hell, with all that is in it, and that was from the bounty of Allāh ﷻ.

He ﷺ continued to a place where he heard the screeching of the pens writing the Divine decree. Then he ﷺ moved further into a place where a cloud shaded him. He began supplicating while in prostration, then the veil was removed and he ﷺ beheld his Lord and Master and heard the Primordial Divine Speech of Allāh. And fifty prayers were ordained for him and his nation, as an obligatory daily practice. This became five daily prayers by the counsel of *al-Kalīm*, Sayyiduna Mūsā. May Allāh's blessings be upon our Prophet and him.

Thereafter, he ﷺ returned to Bayt al-Maqdis and mounted the Burāq once again and returned to the Ḥarām of Makka. The disbelievers denied him, but *al-Ṣiddīq* (Abū Bakr) ؓ attested to his journey, as Allāh had guided him and given him success to do so. It is due to this he is called '*al-Ṣiddīq*' (The Truthful), and he reached the rank of *Ṣiddīqiyya* (spiritual rank under that of Prophethood). May Allāh be pleased with him and with Sayyiduna 'Umar, Sayyiduna 'Uthmān, Sayyiduna 'Alī and all the companions; as well as with Sayyiduna Ḥasan and Sayyiduna Ḥusayn, and their progeny along with their mother, and all their brothers and sisters, and all the *Ahl al-Bayt* of the Messenger of Allāh ﷺ. Upon them all be the blessings of Allāh.

السَّمَاءِ الثَّالِثَةِ وَجَدَ سَيِّدَنَا يُوسُفَ عَلَيْهِ السَّلَامُ الَّذِى أَعْطَاهُ اللهُ شَطْرَ الْحُسْنِ ذَا الْمَحَاسِنِ الْبَهِيَّةِ ، وَفِى السَّمَاءِ الرَّابِعَةِ وَجَدَ سَيِّدَنَا إِدْرِيسَ الَّذِى رَفَعَهُ اللهُ مَكَاناً عَلِيًّا وَعَلَّاهُ ، وَفِى السَّمَاءِ الْخَامِسَةِ وَجَدَ سَيِّدَنَا هَارُونَ الْمُحَبَّبَ عِنْدَ الْأُمَّةِ الْإِسْرَائِيلِيَّةِ ، وَفِى السَّمَاءِ السَّادِسَةِ وَجَدَ سَيِّدَنَا مُوسَى بْنَ عِمْرَانَ عَلَيْهِ السَّلَامُ الَّذِى رَدَّهُ لِتَخْفِيفِ الصَّلَاةِ ، وَفِى السَّمَاءِ السَّابِعَةِ وَجَدَ سَيِّدَنَا إِبْرَاهِيمَ مُتَّكِئاً إِلَى الْبَيْتِ الْمَعْمُورِ بِالْمَلَائِكَةِ النُّورَانِيَّةِ ، وَقَالَ لَهُ : يَا مُحَمَّدُ أَقْرِئْ أُمَّتَكَ مِنِّى السَّلَامَ ، فَعَلَى نَبِيِّنَا وَعَلَيْهِ أَفْضَلُ صَلَاةٍ وَأَتَمُّ سَلَامٍ يَفُوحُ فِى الْكَوْنِ شَذَاهُ، ثُمَّ رَأَى صَلَّى اللهُ عَلَيْهِ وَسَلَّمَ سِدْرَةَ الْمُنْتَهَى الَّتِى تَنْتَهِى إِلَيْهَا الْأَوَامِرُ الْإِلَهِيَّةُ ،

ثُمَّ رَأَى صَلَّى اللهُ عَلَيْهِ وَسَلَّمَ الْجَنَّةَ بِمَا فِيهَا ، وَالنَّارَ وَمَا فِيهَا ، وَذَلِكَ مِنْ فَضْلِ اللهِ ، ثُمَّ سَارَ صَلَّى اللهُ عَلَيْهِ وَسَلَّمَ إِلَى مَكَانٍ سَمِعَ فِيهِ صَرِيرَ الْأَقْلَامِ بِالْمَقَادِيرِ الْإِلَهِيَّةِ ، ثُمَّ سَارَ صَلَّى اللهُ عَلَيْهِ وَسَلَّمَ إِلَى مَكَانٍ أَظَلَّتْهُ فِيهِ غَمَامَةٌ فَابْتَهَلَ سَاجِداً فَكُشِفَ لَهُ الْحِجَابُ وَرَأَى رَبَّهُ وَمَوْلَاهُ وَأَسْمَعَهُ سُبْحَانَهُ وَتَعَالَى كَلَامُهُ الْقَدِيمَ وَفَرَضَ عَلَيْهِ وَعَلَى أُمَّتِهِ خَمْسِينَ صَلَاةً فَرْضِيَّةً ، ثُمَّ صَارَتْ خَمْساً بِمُرَاجَعَةِ الْكَلِيمِ سَيِّدِنَا مُوسَى عَلَى نَبِيِّنَا وَعَلَيْهِ صَلَوَاتُ اللهِ ،

ثُمَّ عَادَ صَلَّى اللهُ عَلَيْهِ وَسَلَّمَ إِلَى بَيْتِ الْمَقْدِسِ وَرَكِبَ الْبُرَاقَ وَوَصَلَ إِلَى الدِّيَارِ الْحَرَمِيَّةِ ، فَكَذَّبَهُ الْكُفَّارُ وَصَدَّقَهُ الصِّدِّيقُ حَيْثُ وَفَّقَهُ اللهُ تَعَالَى لِذَلِكَ وَهَدَاهُ ،

O Allāh send blessings, peace and abundance on our liege and master, Muḥammad, the best of creation, and on his family, in every glance and breath, as many times as all that is contained in the knowledge of Allāh.

وَمِنْ أَجْلِ ذَلِكَ سُمِّيَ الصِّدِّيق وَنَالَ رُتْبَةَ الصِّدِّيقِيَّةِ رَضِيَ اللهُ عَنْهُ وَعَنْ سَيِّدِنَا عُمَرَ وَعَنْ سَيِّدِنَا عُثْمَانَ وَعَنْ سَيِّدِنَا عَلِيٍّ وَجَمِيعِ الصَّحَابَةِ عَلَيْهِمْ رِضْوَانُ اللهِ، وَعَنْ سَيِّدِنَا الْحَسَنِ وَسَيِّدِنَا الْحُسَيْنِ وَمَا تَنَاسَلَ مِنْهُمَا مِنَ الذُّرِّيَّةِ، وَعَنْ أُمِّهِمَا وَأَخَوَاتِهِمَا وَجَمِيعِ أَهْلِ بَيْتِ رَسُولِ اللهِ وَعَلَيْهِمْ صَلَوَاتُ اللهِ،

﴿اللَّهُمَّ صَلِّ وَسَلِّمْ وَبَارِكْ عَلَى سَيِّدِنَا وَمَوْلَانَا مُحَمَّدٍ خَيْرِ الْبَرِيَّةِ،
وَعَلَى آلِهِ فِي كُلِّ لَمْحَةٍ وَنَفَسٍ عَدَدَ مَا وَسِعَهُ عِلْمُ اللهِ﴾

CHAPTER 15

His ﷺ Hijra (Migration)

The Messenger of Allāh ﷺ was patient with the harm directed to him from the polytheists. He would call them with guidance, towards the Muḥammadan Sharīʿa, until Allāh ﷻ gave him permission to migrate to Ṭayba (Madīna), which is the most beloved land to Allāh. The one who accompanied him ﷺ in the blessed migration was he who attained the rank of the Ṣiddīqiyya, the most virtuous of the companions, Sayyiduna Abū Bakr, al-Ṣiddīq ؓ.

There appeared many miracles during the migration which are narrated with authentic chains. Such as: the spider's web, the pigeon's egg, the veiling of the eyes of the disbelievers from seeing him ﷺ, the abundant milk from the goat that belonged to Umm Maʿbad ؓ, which had not [previously produced] a single drop of milk, and the hooves of Surāqa b. Juʿshum's horse, which sank in the ground when he came near to the beloved of Allāh, His chosen one ﷺ.

Allāh ﷻ, turned the disbelievers away from him ﷺ with total failure on their part, and Allāh ﷻ, delivered His Prophet ﷺ with safety and peace, and He preserved him and looked after him ﷺ.

O Allāh send blessings, peace and abundance on our liege and master, Muḥammad, the best of creation, and on his family, in every glance and breath, as many times as all that is contained in the knowledge of Allāh.

الفصل الخامس عشر

فِي هِجْرَتِهِ صَلَّى اللهُ عَلَيْهِ وَسَلَّمَ

وَكَانَ صَلَّى اللهُ عَلَيْهِ وَسَلَّمَ عَظِيمَ الصَّبْرِ عَلَى أَذَى الْمُشْرِكِينَ لَهُ وَيَدْعُو لَهُمْ بِالْهِدَايَةِ إِلَى الشَّرِيعَةِ الْمُحَمَّدِيَّةِ ، حَتَّى أَذِنَ اللهُ تَعَالَى لَهُ بِالْهِجْرَةِ إِلَى طَيْبَةَ الَّتِي هِيَ أَحَبُّ الْبِلَادِ إِلَى اللهِ ، وَكَانَ رَفِيقُهُ صَلَّى اللهُ عَلَيْهِ وَسَلَّمَ فِي هِجْرَتِهِ الْمُبَارَكَةِ ذَا الْمَنْزِلَةِ الصِّدِّيقِيَّةِ ، أَفْضَلَ الصَّحَابَةِ سَيِّدَنَا أَبَا بَكْرٍ الصِّدِّيقَ الَّذِي رَضِيَ اللهُ عَنْهُ وَأَرْضَاهُ ، وَقَدْ ظَهَرَتْ لَهُ صَلَّى اللهُ عَلَيْهِ وَسَلَّمَ فِي طَرِيقِ هِجْرَتِهِ مُعْجِزَاتٌ صَحِيحَةٌ مَرْوِيَّةٌ ، كَنَسْجِ الْعَنْكَبُوتِ ، وَبَيْضِ الْحَمَامَةِ ، وَحَجْبِ أَبْصَارِ الْكَفَرَةِ عَنْ مَرْآهُ ، وَدَرِّ شَاةِ أُمِّ مَعْبَدٍ الَّتِي مَا بِهَا قَطْرَةٌ لَبَنِيَّةٌ ، وَقَدْ سَاخَتْ قَوَائِمُ فَرَسِ سُرَاقَةَ بْنِ جُعْشُمٍ لَمَّا دَنَا مِنْ حَبِيبِ اللهِ وَمُصْطَفَاهُ ، وَرَدَّ اللهُ تَعَالَى عَنْهُ صَلَّى اللهُ عَلَيْهِ وَسَلَّمَ الْكُفَّارَ بِالْخَيْبَةِ الْخِذْلَانِيَّةِ ، وَنَجَّى اللهُ تَعَالَى نَبِيَّهُ صَلَّى اللهُ عَلَيْهِ وَسَلَّمَ بِالْحِفْظِ وَالسَّلَامَةِ وَحَفِظَهُ وَتَوَلَّاهُ ،

﴿اللَّهُمَّ صَلِّ وَسَلِّمْ وَبَارِكْ عَلَى سَيِّدِنَا وَمَوْلَانَا مُحَمَّدٍ خَيْرِ الْبَرِيَّةِ،
وَعَلَى آلِهِ فِي كُلِّ لَمْحَةٍ وَنَفَسٍ عَدَدَ مَا وَسِعَهُ عِلْمُ اللهِ﴾

CHAPTER 16

Entry into al-Madīna al-Munawwara

Seventy or more people from the tribes of *Aws* and *Khazraj*, came to the Prophet ﷺ and believed in him ﷺ. So he ﷺ sent twelve representatives to teach them Qurʾān, fiqh and related matters. Thus, many people believed in him ﷺ and Islām spread in the various areas of Yathrib.

He ﷺ arrived in Madīna on the 12th Rabīʿ al-Awwal, which corresponds to his birthday as we have mentioned in the beginning. When he ﷺ entered Madīna, the people received him with utmost joy and happiness, and with poetry in praise of him. When the people approached to take the reins of the camel, he ﷺ said, "Leave her, for indeed she is under a command." The camel then came to the place of Masjid al-Nabawī, known as *Mabrak al-Nāqa* (the place of the Camel), and she knelt with the permission of Allāh. Sayyiduna Abū Ayyūb al-Anṣārī ﵁ took his ﷺ belongings to his house with joy and happiness, and with good intentions.

During this time everyone was saying, "O Messenger of Allāh, be our guest!" He replied, "Where are my belongings?" Sayyiduna Abū Ayyūb al-Anṣārī ﵁ upon hearing this said, "It is with me, O Messenger of Allāh." The Prophet ﷺ said, "The man stays wherever his belongings stay." How fortunate and blessed is Sayyiduna Abū Ayyūb al-Anṣārī ﵁! Thereafter, he ﷺ built the Masjid and the revelation continued with the rulings of the Sharīʿa.

الفصل السادس عشر

فِي دُخُولِهِ صَلَّى اللهُ عَلَيْهِ وَسَلَّمَ الْمَدِينَةَ الْمُنَوَّرَةَ

وَكَانَ قَدْ جَاءَهُ صَلَّى اللهُ عَلَيْهِ وَسَلَّمَ مَا يَزِيدُ عَلَى السَّبْعِينَ مِنَ الْأَوْسِ وَالْقَبِيلَةِ الْخَزْرَجِيَّةِ ، فَآمَنُوا بِهِ صَلَّى اللهُ عَلَيْهِ وَسَلَّمَ فَبَعَثَ صَلَّى اللهُ عَلَيْهِ وَسَلَّمَ اثْنَى عَشَرَ نَقِيبًا يُعَلِّمُونَهُمُ الْقُرْآنَ وَالْفِقْهَ وَمَا وَالاهُ ، فَآمَنَ بِهِ صَلَّى اللهُ عَلَيْهِ وَسَلَّمَ خَلْقٌ كَثِيرٌ ، وَانْتَشَرَ الْإِسْلَامُ فِي الأَرَاضِي الْيَثْرِبِيَّةِ ، وَقَدِمَ صَلَّى اللهُ عَلَيْهِ وَسَلَّمَ عَلَيْهِمُ الْمَدِينَةَ يَوْمَ الإِثْنَيْنِ الثَّانِي عَشَرَ مِنْ رَبِيعٍ الْأَوَّلِ الَّذِي هُوَ تَارِيخُ وِلَادَتِهِ كَمَا رَوَيْنَاهُ ، وَلَمَّا دَخَلَ صَلَّى اللهُ عَلَيْهِ وَسَلَّمَ الْمَدِينَةَ اسْتَقْبَلَهُ أَهْلُهَا بِالْبِشْرِ وَالسُّرُورِ ، وَالْمَدَائِحِ الشِّعْرِيَّةِ ، وَلَمَّا أَرَادُوا أَنْ يَأْخُذُوا بِزِمَامِ النَّاقَةِ قَالَ صَلَّى اللهُ عَلَيْهِ وَسَلَّمَ : دَعُوهَا فَإِنَّهَا مَأْمُورَةٌ ، فَجَاءَتْ عِنْدَ مَكَانِ الْمَسْجِدِ النَّبَوِيِّ الْمُسَمَّى الْآنَ بِمَبْرَكِ النَّاقَةِ وَبَرَكَتْ بِإِذْنِ اللهِ ، فَأَخَذَ أَبُو أَيُّوبَ الْأَنْصَارِيُّ رَضِيَ اللهُ عَنْهُ رَحْلَهُ صَلَّى اللهُ عَلَيْهِ وَسَلَّمَ إِلَى بَيْتِهِ بِالْفَرَحِ وَالسُّرُورِ ، وَحُسْنِ النِّيَّةِ ، وَكُلٌّ يَقُولُ تَنْزِلُ عِنْدِي يَا رَسُولَ اللهِ ، فَقَالَ صَلَّى اللهُ عَلَيْهِ وَسَلَّمَ: أَيْنَ الرَّحْلُ؟ فَقَالَ أَبُو أَيُّوبَ : هُوَ عِنْدِي يَا رَسُولَ اللهِ ، فَقَالَ صَلَّى اللهُ عَلَيْهِ وَسَلَّمَ: يَبِيتُ الرَّجُلُ حَيْثُ بَاتَ رَحْلُهُ ، فَيَا سَعْدَ أَبِي أَيُّوبَ وَيَا بُشْرَاهُ ،

The *Muhājirūn* (the Migrants) and the *Anṣār* (the Helpers) came to the Messenger of Allāh ﷺ, leaving behind their dwelling places and belongings. The Muhājirūn came for the sake of Allāh and His Messenger ﷺ, with determination and strength, carrying famous Indian-steel swords. The army was vigorous; brandishing their weapons and their strength.

O Allāh send blessings, peace and abundance on our liege and master, Muḥammad, the best of creation, and on his family, in every glance and breath, as many times as all that is contained in the knowledge of Allāh.

ثُمَّ بَنَى صَلَّى اللهُ عَلَيْهِ وَسَلَّمَ الْمَسْجِدَ ، وَتَتَابَعَ الْوَحْيُ بِالْأَحْكَامِ الشَّرْعِيَّةِ ، وَجَاءَهُ الْمُهَاجِرُونَ وَالْأَنْصَارُ ، وَقَدْ تَرَكَ كُلٌّ وَطَنَهُ وَمَأْوَاهُ ، جَاءُوا مُهَاجِرِينَ لِلهِ تَعَالَى وَلِرَسُولِهِ صَلَّى اللهُ عَلَيْهِ وَسَلَّمَ بِعَزِيمَةٍ وَقُوَّةٍ يَحْمِلُونَ السُّيُوفَ الْهِنْدِيَّةَ، فَقَوِيَ الْجَيْشُ بِأَخْطَرِ سِلَاحٍ وَأَقْوَاهُ ،

﴿اللّٰهُمَّ صَلِّ وَسَلِّمْ وَبَارِكْ عَلَى سَيِّدِنَا وَمَوْلَانَا مُحَمَّدٍ خَيْرِ الْبَرِيَّةِ،
وَعَلَى آلِهِ فِي كُلِّ لَمْحَةٍ وَنَفَسٍ عَدَدَ مَا وَسِعَهُ عِلْمُ اللهِ﴾

CHAPTER 17

Expeditions and the Conquest of Makka

The Prophet ﷺ strove in the path of Allāh for the upliftment of His Word in every major or minor expedition. Wherever he ﷺ went, he had victory and support against those who fought against and showed enmity to him. From the most well-known of his expeditions was the Battle of Badr, where the army of angels descended. The expedition which Allāh ﷻ informed the *mujāhidīn* about when He said: "Do as you please, for certainly I have forgiven you." Due to this, each of them were given success [from Allāh] to achieve goodness and have a good ending.

The Muslims killed seventy of the leaders of the disbelievers and imprisoned another seventy of them. They obtained the pinnacle of victory. Then Allāh ﷻ gave permission for the conquest of Makka and the vicinity surrounding the Ḥarām. So the Prophet ﷺ, together with ten thousand of those by whom Allāh assisted and strengthened His religion, entered Makka and removed the idols that the Arabs worshipped in the days of ignorance. The *Khuzā'a* tribe had an idol made of glass which they placed on top of the Ka'ba. The Prophet ﷺ ordered Sayyiduna 'Alī, may Allāh ennoble his countenance, to place his feet on his ﷺ blessed shoulders and climb up the Ka'ba. The Prophet ﷺ stood while Sayyiduna 'Alī ؓ went up and took hold of the idol and smashed it to the ground with

الفصل السابع عشر

جِهَادُهُ صَلَّى اللهُ عَلَيْهِ وَسَلَّمَ وَفَتْحُ مَكَّةَ

وَجَاهَدَ صَلَّى اللهُ عَلَيْهِ وَسَلَّمَ فِي سَبِيلِ اللهِ تَعَالَى لِإِعْلَاءِ كَلِمَتِهِ فِي غَزْوَةٍ وَسَرِيَّةٍ، وَكَانَ صَلَّى اللهُ عَلَيْهِ وَسَلَّمَ حَيْثُ مَا تَوَجَّهَ لَهُ الْغَلَبَةُ وَالنَّصْرُ عَلَى كُلِّ مَنْ قَاتَلَهُ وَعَادَاهُ ،

وَمِنْ أَشْهَرِ غَزَوَاتِهِ بَدْرٌ الَّتِي نَزَلَتْ فِيهَا الْجُيُوشُ الْمَلَكِيَّةُ ، الَّتِي اطَّلَعَ اللهُ فِيهَا عَلَى الْمُجَاهِدِينَ وَقَالَ : اعْمَلُوا مَا شِئْتُمْ فَقَدْ غَفَرْتُ لَكُمْ ، فَكُلٌّ وُفِّقَ لِلْخَيْرِ بِذَلِكَ وَحَسُنَتْ عُقْبَاهُ ، وَقَتَلَ الْمُسْلِمُونَ فِيهَا سَبْعِينَ مِنْ رُؤَسَاءِ الْفِئَةِ الْكُفْرِيَّةِ ، كَمَا أَسَرُوا سَبْعِينَ مِنْهُمْ وَقَدْ بَلَغَ النَّصْرُ مُنْتَهَاهُ ، حَتَّى أَذِنَ اللهُ تَعَالَى بِفَتْحِ مَكَّةَ وَالدِّيَارِ الْحَرَمِيَّةِ ، فَجَاءَهَا صَلَّى اللهُ عَلَيْهِ وَسَلَّمَ مَعَ عَشَرَةِ آلَافٍ مِمَّنْ أَيَّدَهُمُ اللهُ بِدِينِهِ وَتَقْوَاهُ ، وَدَخَلَ مَكَّةَ ، وَأَزَالَ الْأَصْنَامَ الَّتِي كَانَتْ تَعْبُدُهَا الْعَرَبُ فِي الْجَاهِلِيَّةِ ، وَكَانَ لِخُزَاعَةَ صَنَمٌ مِنْ زُجَاجٍ فَوْقَ سَطْحِ الْكَعْبَةِ رَفَعْتُهُ ، فَكَانَ إِلَى الدَّمَارِ مُنْتَهَاهُ ، فَأَمَرَ النَّبِيُّ صَلَّى اللهُ عَلَيْهِ وَسَلَّمَ سَيِّدَنَا عَلِيًّا رَضِيَ اللهُ عَنْهُ وَكَرَّمَ اللهُ وَجْهَهُ أَنْ يَضَعَ قَدَمَيْهِ عَلَى كَتِفَيْهِ الشَّرِيفَتَيْنِ ، ثُمَّ وَقَفَ

his mighty hands, shattering it into pieces. How ignorant is the one that would take an idol as a deity, worshipping and calling on it for their needs! When the idol was broken, the face of the Prophet ﷺ began radiating with joy and delight at the removal of polytheism and idol worship. The Prophet ﷺ kissed the Black Stone and then made *ṭawāf* of the Ancient House, and praised Allāh Most High and exclaimed "*Labbayk*!" He ﷺ was making ṭawāf while the blessed *Ṣaḥāba* gathered around him like shining stars. Abū Sufyān ؓ, who was standing nearby, said to himself, "How did this man (Prophet Muḥammad) defeat me?" The Prophet ﷺ placed his noble hand on the chest of Abū Sufyān ؓ and said, "I have defeated you by [the help of] Allāh!"

He ﷺ announced to the people of Makka: "Go! You are free!" and he spread to them the mercy of the Most Merciful. The *muʾadhdhin* called the adhān, the House of Allāh was illuminated, and the worshippers established their place of prayer. *Sūra al-Naṣr* was revealed to him ﷺ, indicating the nearness of his [worldly] departure and his entry into the Gardens of Paradise; so that he may live eternally with the prophets and messengers, that were present at the occasion of Isrāʾ and Mi'raj; the blessings and peace of Allāh be upon them all.

O Allāh send blessings, peace and abundance on our liege and master, Muḥammad, the best of creation, and on his family, in every glance and breath, as many times as all that is contained in the knowledge of Allāh.

النَّبِيُّ صَلَّى اللهُ عَلَيْهِ وَسَلَّمَ فَأَخَذَ سَيِّدُنَا عَلِيٌّ رَضِيَ اللهُ عَنْهُ الصَّنَمَ وَضَرَبَ بِهِ الْأَرْضَ بِيَدِهِ الْقَوِيَّةِ ، فَتَحَطَّمَ تَحْطِيماً ، فَمَا أَجْهَلَ مَنِ اتَّخَذَهُ إِلَهاً وَعَبَدَهُ وَنَادَاهُ، فَلَمَّا حُطِّمَ تَهَلَّلَ وَجْهُ النَّبِيِّ صَلَّى اللهُ عَلَيْهِ وَسَلَّمَ بِالسُّرُورِ وَالْفَرَحِ لِإِزَالَةِ الشِّرْكِ وَالْوَثَنِيَّةِ ، وَقَبَّلَ الْحَجَرَ ، وَطَافَ بِالْبَيْتِ الْعَتِيقِ ، وَحَمِدَ اللهَ تَعَالَى وَلَبَّاهُ ،

وَكَانَ صَلَّى اللهُ عَلَيْهِ وَسَلَّمَ يَطُوفُ بِالْبَيْتِ وَالصَّحَابَةُ رَضِيَ اللهُ عَنْهُمْ حَوْلَهُ كَالنُّجُومِ الزُّهْرِيَّةِ ، وَكَانَ أَبُو سُفْيَانَ وَاقِفاً ، وَهُوَ يَقُولُ فِي نَفْسِهِ : بِمَ غَلَبَنِي هَذَا الرَّجُلُ ؟ فَوَضَعَ النَّبِيُّ صَلَّى اللهُ عَلَيْهِ وَسَلَّمَ يَدَهُ الشَّرِيفَةَ عَلَى صَدْرِهِ ، وَقَالَ لَهُ : غَلَبْتُكَ بِاللهِ ، وَقَالَ لِأَهْلِ مَكَّةَ : اذْهَبُوا فَأَنْتُمُ الطُّلَقَاءُ ، وَعَمَّهُمْ صَلَّى اللهُ عَلَيْهِ وَسَلَّمَ بِرَحْمَتِهِ الرَّحْمَانِيَّةِ ، وَأَذَّنَ الْمُؤَذِّنُ ، وَابْتَهَجَ الْبَيْتُ وَعَمَرَ الْمُصَلِّي مُصَلَّاهُ، وَنَزَلَتْ عَلَيْهِ صَلَّى اللهُ عَلَيْهِ وَسَلَّمَ سُورَةُ النَّصْرِ تُشِيرُ إِلَى دُنُوِّ أَجَلِهِ صَلَّى اللهُ عَلَيْهِ وَسَلَّمَ ، وَانْتِقَالِهِ إِلَى الرَّوْضَةِ الْجِنَانِيَّةِ ، لِيَحْيَا حَيَاةَ الْخُلُودِ مَعَ النَّبِيِّينَ وَالْمُرْسَلِينَ صَلَوَاتُ اللهِ وَسَلَامُهُ عَلَيْهِمْ مِمَّنْ حَضَرَ لَيْلَةَ مِعْرَاجِهِ وَمَسْرَاهُ ،

﴿اللَّهُمَّ صَلِّ وَسَلِّمْ وَبَارِكْ عَلَى سَيِّدِنَا وَمَوْلَانَا مُحَمَّدٍ خَيْرِ الْبَرِيَّةِ،
وَعَلَى آلِهِ فِي كُلِّ لَمْحَةٍ وَنَفَسٍ عَدَدَ مَا وَسِعَهُ عِلْمُ اللهِ﴾

CHAPTER 18

Concerning His Physical Appearance ﷺ

Now comes the moment for the lovers to hear the attributes of their Beloved ﷺ, such noble attributes that no one else of mankind can achieve.

O those who are present! Prepare your hearts to witness him ﷺ, and perhaps your souls will get a glimpse of his astonishing radiance ﷺ.

The Ṣaḥāba ؓ have described him ﷺ in the authentic narrations. His complexion was fair, tinged with redness. His noble face would emanate radiant lights. When he spoke, a light shone from his honorable mouth for the one who heard and saw him ﷺ. He was of average height [among his people] but inclined towards being a tall person. When he walked with others who were taller, his noble head was higher than them to onlookers (as one of the Prophetic miracles). He had a large head with slightly wavy hair. His hair would not go [much] below his earlobes. When his blessed hair used to be trimmed, he would order his hair to be distributed amongst the Ṣaḥāba ؓ, those of high aspiration. For whoever received a strand of his hair, it was more beloved to him than this world and all that it contains. This is how it is mentioned by Imām al-Bukhari ؒ in his compilation, in which he gathered reliable narrators. He had a luminous complexion, broad forehead, and thick eyebrows arched like the crescent moon.

الفصل الثامن عشر

فِي وَصْفِهِ صَلَّى اللهُ عَلَيْهِ وَسَلَّمَ

وَقَدْ آنَ لِلْمُحِبِّينَ أَنْ يَسْمَعُوا أَوْصَافَ حَبِيبِهِمْ صَلَّى اللهُ عَلَيْهِ وَسَلَّمَ الَّتِي مَا نَالَهَا أَحَدٌ مِنَ الْأُمَّةِ الْإِنْسَانِيَّةِ ، فَهَيِّئُوا قُلُوبَكُمْ يَا حَاضِرِينَ لِمُشَاهَدَتِهِ صَلَّى اللهُ عَلَيْهِ وَسَلَّمَ فَعَسَى أَرْوَاحُكُمْ أَنْ تَلْمَحَ بَدِيعَ سَنَاهُ ،

وَقَدْ وَصَفَهُ صَلَّى اللهُ عَلَيْهِ وَسَلَّمَ الصَّحَابَةُ رَضِيَ اللهُ عَنْهُمْ فِي الْأَحَادِيثِ الصَّحِيحَةِ الْمَرْوِيَّةِ ، أَنَّهُ كَانَ أَبْيَضَ اللَّوْنِ مُشْرَباً بِحُمْرَةٍ تَعْلُو وَجْهَهُ الشَّرِيفَ أَنْوَارٌ نُورَانِيَّةٌ ، إِذَا تَكَلَّمَ خَرَجَ مِنْ فَمِهِ الشَّرِيفِ نُورٌ لِمَنْ سَمِعَ كَلَامَهُ وَرَوَاهُ ، مَرْبُوعَ الْقَامَةِ إِلَى الطُّولِ أَمْيَلُ ، إِذَا مَشَى مَعَ أَطْوَلِ النَّاسِ عَلَا رَأْسُهُ الشَّرِيفُ عَلَيْهِ لِمَنْ رَآهُ ، عَظِيمَ الرَّأْسِ رَجِلَ الشَّعْرِ لَا يَطُولُ شَعْرُهُ عَلَى شَحْمَةِ أُذُنَيْهِ ، إِذَا حَلَقَهُ أَمَرَ بِتَقْسِيمِهِ عَلَى أَصْحَابِهِ ذَوِي الْهِمَّةِ الْعَلِيَّةِ ، فَمَنْ أَخَذَ شَعْرَةً كَانَتْ أَحَبَّ إِلَيْهِ مِنَ الدُّنْيَا وَمَا فِيهَا ، كَمَا أَخْرَجَ ذَلِكَ الْبُخَارِيُّ فِي صَحِيحِهِ الَّذِي جَمَعَ ثِقَاةَ الرُّوَاةِ ، أَزْهَرَ اللَّوْنِ ، وَاسِعَ الْجَبِينِ ، أَزَجَّ الْحَوَاجِبِ فِي صُورَةٍ هِلَالِيَّةٍ، أَقْنَى الْعِرْنِينِ ، أَيْ مُرْتَفِعَ الْأَنْفِ مَعَ الْجَمَالِ وَالْمُسَاوَاةِ ، كَثَّ اللِّحْيَةِ، أَيْ عَظِيمَةً

He ﷺ had a slightly raised nose with beauty and symmetry. He had a copious beard, meaning a large, pitch black and clean beard. He had smooth cheeks, the white part of his blessed eyes were immaculately white and his pupils were pitch black. His eyes looked as if they were naturally applied with ithmid kuḥl. He had a wide mouth and his teeth were lustrous, meaning they were bright and shining. His teeth were perfectly spaced out and according to the Arabs, this is an indication that the speaker is able to compose his words and convey his speech with eloquence.

He ﷺ had a thin line of hair on his noble chest, which is known as al-Masrūba, which shone and was like soft silk. He had a moderately white neck, long and graceful like that of a statue. He had heavy joints of the bones, meaning his bones were broad in between the shoulders. He had a strong body like that of a lion. His blessed stomach and chest were in line (the stomach was not protruding) for he ﷺ was perfect in form, character, and all virtues. His shoulders and arms had hair but his chest had no hair. His physical fragrance would surpass the aroma of Indian musk and was more fragrant. The waste that was expelled from his body was sweeter than perfume. He ﷺ would take extra care in purifying himself, out of veneration of the One who selected and chose him.

The palms of his hands were wide, and how generous they were, owing to his charitable giving in the way of his Master. His palms were softer than silk to the touch. How fortunate is he who shook them and kissed those Muḥammadan hands!

It has been reported by Imām Abū Dāwūd ؓ in his Sunan, that when the delegation of ʿAbd al-Qays came, they rushed to kiss his hands and feet, out of love and yearning and for having the honor to meet him ﷺ.

He would greet the one who met him, smiling and with salām; looking at them with a gaze of love and the Muḥammadan com-

سَوْدَاءَ نَقِيَّةً ، سَهْلَ الْخَدَّيْنِ ، أَدْعَجَ الْعَيْنَيْنِ ، أَيْ شَدِيدَ بَيَاضِ الْعَيْنَيْنِ وَشَدِيدَ سَوَادِهِمَا ، وَقَدْ كُحِلَتْ بِإِثْمِدِ الْقُدْرَةِ عَيْنَاهُ ، وَاسِعَ الْفَمِ ، أَشْنَبَ الْأَسْنَانِ ، أَيْ لَهَا لَمَعَانٌ وَبَرِيقٌ وَصِفَاتٌ نُورَانِيَّةٌ ، أَفْلَجَ الْأَسْنَانِ ، وَذَلِكَ يَدُلُّ عِنْدَ الْعَرَبِ عَلَى فَصَاحَةِ الْمُتَكَلِّمِ إِذَا نَثَرَ كَلَامَهُ وَأَلْقَاهُ ،

لَهُ شَعْرٌ دَقِيقٌ عَلَى صَدْرِهِ الشَّرِيفِ يُسَمَّى الْمَسْرُبَةَ ذُو لُيُونَةٍ سُنْدُسِيَّةٍ ، أَبْيَضَ الْعُنُقِ مُعْتَدِلَهُ كَأَنَّهُ جِيدُ دُمْيَةٍ ، ضَخْمَ الْكَرَادِيسِ ، أَيْ رُءُوسِ الْعِظَامِ بَعِيدَ مَا بَيْنَ الْمَنْكِبَيْنِ ، بَادِناً مُتَمَاسِكاً ذَا قُوَّةٍ أَسَدِيَّةٍ ، سَوَاءَ الْبَطْنِ وَالصَّدْرِ ، لِأَنَّهُ صَلَّى اللهُ عَلَيْهِ وَسَلَّمَ كَامِلُ الْخَلْقِ وَالْخُلُقِ فِي جَمِيعِ مَزَايَاهُ ، أَشْعَرَ الْمَنْكِبَيْنِ وَالذِّرَاعَيْنِ ، عَارِيَ الثَّدْيَيْنِ ، أَيْ لَا شَعْرَ فِيهِمَا ، ذَا رَوَائِحَ تَفُوقُ رَوَائِحَ الْمِسْكِ الْهِنْدِيَّةَ ، وَرِيحُهُ صَلَّى اللهُ عَلَيْهِ وَسَلَّمَ أَطْيَبُ مِنَ الْمِسْكِ ، وَفَضَلَاتُهُ الَّتِي تَخْرُجُ مِنْهُ صَلَّى اللهُ عَلَيْهِ وَسَلَّمَ أَطْيَبُ مِنَ الْعِطْرِ ، وَإِنَّمَا يَتَطَهَّرُ تَعَبُّدًا لِمَنِ اخْتَارَهُ وَاصْطَفَاهُ ،

رَحْبَ الرَّاحَتَيْنِ، فَكَمْ جَادَ بِهِمَا وَتَصَدَّقَ فِي سَبِيلِ مَوْلَاهُ ، كَفُّهُ أَلْيَنُ مِنَ الْحَرِيرِ لَمْسُهُ ، فَطُوبَى لِمَنْ صَافَحَ وَقَبَّلَ تِلْكَ الْيَدَ الْمُحَمَّدِيَّةَ ، وَقَدْ أَخْرَجَ أَبُو دَاوُدَ فِي سُنَنِهِ أَنَّ وَفْدَ عَبْدِ الْقَيْسِ ابْتَدَرُوا يَدَيْهِ وَرِجْلَيْهِ صَلَّى اللهُ عَلَيْهِ وَسَلَّمَ فَقَبَّلُوهَا حُبًّا وَشَوْقاً وَتَكْرِيماً لِمُحَيَّاهُ ،

يَبْدَأُ مَنْ لَقِيَهُ بِالسَّلَامِ مُبْتَسِماً، نَاظِراً لَهُ بِنَظَرَاتِ الْحُبِّ ذَاتِ الرَّأْفَةِ الْمُحَمَّدِيَّةِ،

passion. No believer ever saw him but their heart would soften, and they would love him and be eager to spend all their time with him ﷺ.

When he ﷺ walked, he lifted his feet firmly as though descending from a high place, and this indicates bodily strength. No one from amongst the Arabs ever wrestled with him except that he ﷺ overpowered them and threw them to the ground.

He ﷺ was always in deep thought and remained silent much, pondering over matters that affect the Islāmic Umma. His voice was audible and his speech could be heard by anyone who desired and intended to hear it.

He ﷺ would often look down due to his modesty for Allāh. His gaze was fixed on the ground more than to the heavens above. Most of his gaze were glances, and he could see those behind him the same as he saw those in front of him; that was not possible for anyone besides him.

Sayyiduna Ḥassān b. Thābit said very eloquently:

> More handsome than you, my eye has never seen,
> More perfect than you, no woman has given birth to,
>
> You have been created free from all defects,
> As if you were created the way you wished!

And al-Būṣīrī, said:

> There is no equal to him in his magnificence,
> in him is the indivisible jewel of beauty.
>
> Like pearls which are well preserved in oysters,
> from the two mines, of his speech and his smiles.

فَمَا رَآهُ مُؤْمِنٌ إِلَّا لَانَ قَلْبُهُ وَأَحَبَّهُ وَتَمَنَّى فِي كُلِّ سَاعَةٍ لُقْيَاهُ ، إِذَا مَشَى يَتَقَلَّعُ فِي مَشْيِهِ كَأَنَّمَا يَنْزِلُ مِنْ مَكَانٍ مُرْتَفِعٍ ، وَذَلِكَ يَدُلُّ عَلَى الْقُوَّةِ الْبَدَنِيَّةِ ، وَمَا صَارَعَهُ أَحَدٌ مِنَ الْعَرَبِ إِلاَّ تَغَلَّبَ عَلَيْهِ صَلَّى اللهُ عَلَيْهِ وَسَلَّمَ وَصَرَعَهُ وَعَلَى الْأَرْضِ أَلْقَاهُ ،

دَائِمَ الْفِكْرِ، كَثِيرَ السُّكُوتِ ، يَهْتَمُّ لِأُمَّتِهِ الْإِسْلَامِيَّةِ ، جَهْوَرِيَّ الصَّوْتِ يَسْمَعُ كَلَامَهُ كُلُّ مَنْ أَرَادَ سَمَاعَهُ وَنَوَاهُ ، سَابِلَ الطَّرْفِ حَيَاءً مِنَ اللهِ تَعَالَى ، نَظَرُهُ إِلَى الْأَرْضِ أَطْوَلُ مِنْ نَظَرِهِ إِلَى السَّمَوَاتِ الْعُلْوِيَّةِ ، أَكْثَرُ نَظَرِهِ الْمُلَاحَظَةُ يَرَى مَنْ خَلْفَهُ كَمَا يَرَى مَنْ أَمَامَهُ ، وَلَمْ يَكُنْ ذَلِكَ لِأَحَدٍ سِوَاهُ ، وَقَدْ أَجَادَ حَسَّانُ بْنُ ثَابِتٍ رَضِيَ اللهُ عَنْهُ حَيْثُ قَالَ:

وَأَجْمَلُ مِنْكَ لَمْ تَرَ قَطُّ عَيْنِي ... وَأَكْمَلُ مِنْكَ لَمْ تَلِدِ النِّسَاءُ
خُلِقْتَ مُبَرَّءًا مِنْ كُلِّ عَيْبٍ ... كَأَنَّكَ قَدْ خُلِقْتَ كَمَا تَشَاءُ

وَقَالَ الْبُوصِيرِي رَحِمَهُ اللهُ :

مُنَزَّهٌ عَنْ شَرِيكٍ فِي مَحَاسِنِهِ ... فَجَوْهَرُ الْحُسْنِ فِيهِ غَيْرُ مُنْقَسِمِ
كَأَنَّمَا اللُّؤْلُؤُ الْمَكْنُونُ فِي صَدَفٍ ... مِنْ مَعْدِنَيْ مَنْطِقٍ مِنْهُ وَمُبْتَسَمِ
أَكْرِمْ بِخَلْقِ نَبِيٍّ زَانَهُ خُلُقٌ ... بِالْحُسْنِ مُشْتَمِلٍ بِالْبِشْرِ مُتَّسِمِ

How noble are the physical qualities of our Prophet ﷺ which are adorned with good character,
Dressed with beauty; and distinguished by pleasant nature.

Like a blooming flower in its freshness and like the moon when it is full in splendor,
And like the ocean in generosity and like time in persistence.

Even when alone, he looks due to his grandeur;
As though he is in the midst of a large army and its retinue.

O our brother! Prepare your heart for his presence ﷺ in this gathering of ours, when we recite the Prophetic biography. Perhaps you may gain your share of what our shaykh, Sayyid Aḥmad b. Idrīs ؓ attained; the one who Allāh is pleased with and whom He pleased.

O Allāh send blessings, peace and abundance on our liege and master, Muḥammad, the best of creation, and on his family, in every glance and breath, as many times as all that is contained in the knowledge of Allāh.

كَالزَّهْـرِ فِى تَـرَفٍ وَالْبَـدْرِ فِى شَرَفٍ   وَالْبَحْـرِ فِى كَـرَمٍ وَالدَّهْـرِ فِى هِمَـمِ
كَأَنَّـهُ وَهْـوَ فَـرْدٌ مِـنْ جَلَالَتِـهِ   فِى عَسْكَرٍ حِينَ تَلْقَاهُ وَفِى حَشَـمِ

فَهَيِّءْ يَا أَخَانَا بِقَلْبِكَ حُضُورَهُ صَلَّى اللهُ عَلَيْهِ وَسَلَّمَ فِى مَجْلِسِنَا هَذَا عِنْدَ تِلَاوَةِ سِيرَتِهِ النَّبَوِيَّةِ ، لَعَلَّكَ أَنْ تَحْظَى بِمَا حَظِيَ بِهِ شَيْخُنَا السَّيِّدُ أَحْمَدُ بْنُ إِدْرِيسَ الَّذِى رَضِيَ اللهُ عَنْهُ وَأَرْضَاهُ ،

﴿اللّٰهُمَّ صَلِّ وَسَلِّمْ وَبَارِكْ عَلَى سَيِّدِنَا وَمَوْلَانَا مُحَمَّدٍ خَيْرِ الْبَرِيَّةِ،
وَعَلَى آلِهِ فِى كُلِّ لَمْحَةٍ وَنَفَسٍ عَدَدَ مَا وَسِعَهُ عِلْمُ اللهِ﴾

CHAPTER 19

His ﷺ Lofty Character

With regards to his noble character, the Prophet ﷺ was the most perfect man in character. He was magnanimous and a noble soul. He would forgive the one who oppressed him and would reconcile with the one who broke ties with him. He would spread his righteousness and generosity. He would repel evil with good and would be patient with hardships. He would not return evil with evil but rather with goodness and mercy.

When the people of al-Ṭāʾif pelted him with stones causing his blessed shin to bleed, the angels sought his permission to destroy them. However, he said, "I hope Allāh will bring forth from their progeny such people who will worship Allāh alone."

He ﷺ pardoned the people of Makka with an all-embracing forgiveness which was unprecedented in the annals of Arabian history.

And Allāh praised his character by saying: *And you (O Muḥammad) possess the loftiest of character.*

How great is this praise and how lofty it is! A man came to him ﷺ and grabbed him violently by his collar, in a rough Bedouin manner. He then released him ﷺ and said, "Give me from the wealth of Allāh, as it does not belong to your father nor your grandfather." The Prophet ﷺ gave him so many sheep that it was enough to free him from poverty and be totally independent from others.

الفصل التاسع عشر

فِي أَخْلَاقِهِ صَلَّى اللهُ عَلَيْهِ وَسَلَّمَ

وَأَمَّا أَخْلَاقِهِ صَلَّى اللهُ عَلَيْهِ وَسَلَّمَ فَكَانَ أَكْمَلَ النَّاسِ أَخْلَاقاً ذَا صَدْرٍ رَحْبٍ وَنَفْسٍ سَنِيَّةٍ ، يَعْفُو عَمَّنْ ظَلَمَهُ ، وَيَصِلُ مَنْ قَطَعَهُ ، وَيُعَمِّمُ بِرَّهُ وَعَطَايَاهُ ، وَيَدْرَأُ بِالْحَسَنَةِ السَّيِّئَةَ ، وَيَصْبِرُ عَلَى الْأَذِيَّةِ ، وَلَا يُقَابِلُ السَّيِّئَةَ بِالسَّيِّئَةِ ، بَلْ بِخَيْرِهِ وَنَدَاهُ ، وَلَمَّا أَدْمَى سَاقَيْهِ الشَّرِيفَتَيْنِ أَهْلُ الطَّائِفِ بِالْإِصَابَاتِ الْحَجَرِيَّةِ ، اسْتَأْذَنَتْهُ صَلَّى اللهُ عَلَيْهِ وَسَلَّمَ الْمَلَائِكَةُ بِإِهْلَاكِهِمْ ، فَقَالَ : أَرْجُو أَنْ يُخْرِجَ اللهُ مِنْ أَصْلَابِهِمْ مَنْ يَعْبُدُ اللهَ ، وَعَفَا صَلَّى اللهُ عَلَيْهِ وَسَلَّمَ عَنْ أَهْلِ مَكَّةَ عَفْواً شَامِلاً لَمْ يَسْبِقْ فِي تَارِيخِ الْأُمَّةِ الْعَرَبِيَّةِ ، وَقَدْ أَثْنَى اللهُ تَعَالَى عَلَى خُلُقِهِ صَلَّى اللهُ عَلَيْهِ وَسَلَّمَ بِقَوْلِهِ : ﴿وَإِنَّكَ لَعَلَى خُلُقٍ عَظِيمٍ﴾ فَمَا أَعْظَمَ هَذَا الثَّنَاءَ وَمَا أَعْلَاهُ ،

وَجَاءَهُ صَلَّى اللهُ عَلَيْهِ وَسَلَّمَ رَجُلٌ وَأَمْسِكَ ، بِجَيْبِهِ وَشَدَّهُ شَدَّةً أَعْرَابِيَّةً ، ثُمَّ أَرْسَلَهُ صَلَّى اللهُ عَلَيْهِ وَسَلَّمَ وَقَالَ : أَعْطِنِي مِنْ مَالِ اللهِ الَّذِي هُوَ لَيْسَ مَالَ أَبِيكَ وَلَا جَدِّكَ ، وَأَعْطَاهُ صَلَّى اللهُ عَلَيْهِ وَسَلَّمَ مِنَ الْغَنَمِ مَا أَذْهَبَ فَقْرَهُ وَأَغْنَاهُ،

On another occasion, he ﷺ was taking a *qaylūla* (afternoon siesta) under the shade of a tree, while his sword was hanging from one of its branches, when one of the polytheists came and grabbed the sword. He ﷺ awoke. The man said, "Who will protect you now from me, O son of ʿAbdullāh?" He ﷺ replied, "My Lord will save me from you, the One who is Eternal." The sword fell from the man's hand, and the Prophet ﷺ took him and threw him to the ground, and asked him, "Who will protect you from me now, O enemy of Allāh?" The man replied, "It is your clemency, O most kind amongst the Arab nation." He ﷺ let go of him; the polytheist proclaimed, "I believe that you are the Messenger of Allāh," then embraced Islām.

O Allāh send blessings, peace and abundance on our liege and master, Muḥammad, the best of creation, and on his family, in every glance and breath, as many times as all that is contained in the knowledge of Allāh.

وَكَانَ صَلَّى اللهُ عَلَيْهِ وَسَلَّمَ قَائِلاً تَحْتَ ظِلِّ شَجَرَةٍ وَقَدْ عَلَّقَ سَيْفَهُ بِفَرْعٍ مِنْ فُرُوعِهَا الشَّوْكِيَّةِ ، وَجَاءَ رَجُلٌ مُشْرِكٌ فَأَخَذَ السَّيْفَ وَأَيْقَظَهُ صَلَّى اللهُ عَلَيْهِ وَسَلَّمَ وَقَالَ : مَنْ يَمْنَعُكَ مِنِّي يَا ابْنَ عَبْدِ اللهِ ؟ ، قَالَ صَلَّى اللهُ عَلَيْهِ وَسَلَّمَ: يَمْنَعُنِي مِنْكَ رَبِّي الَّذِى لَهُ الْأَبَدِيَّةُ ، فَطَارَ السَّيْفُ مِنْ يَدِهِ ، فَأَخَذَهُ النَّبِيُّ صَلَّى اللهُ عَلَيْهِ وَسَلَّمَ وَأَلْقَى الْمُشْرِكَ عَلَى الْأَرْضِ ، وَقَالَ لَهُ صَلَّى اللهُ عَلَيْهِ وَسَلَّمَ: مَنْ يَمْنَعُكَ مِنِّي يَا عَدُوَّ اللهِ ؟ ، فَقَالَ الْمُشْرِكُ : يَمْنَعُنِي مِنْكَ حِلْمُكَ يَا أَكْرَمَ الْأُمَّةِ الْعَرَبِيَّةِ ، فَتَرَكَهُ النَّبِيُّ صَلَّى اللهُ عَلَيْهِ وَسَلَّمَ ، فَقَالَ الْمُشْرِكُ: آمَنْتُ أَنَّكَ رَسُولُ اللهِ ،

﴿اللَّهُمَّ صَلِّ وَسَلِّمْ وَبَارِكْ عَلَى سَيِّدِنَا وَمَوْلَانَا مُحَمَّدٍ خَيْرِ الْبَرِيَّةِ،
وَعَلَى آلِهِ فِي كُلِّ لَمْحَةٍ وَنَفَسٍ عَدَدَ مَا وَسِعَهُ عِلْمُ اللهِ﴾

CHAPTER 20

Seeking Means Through him ﷺ

As for taking the Prophet ﷺ as a means [of intercession], the scholars of the past and present are in unanimous agreement that it is permissible, without any doubt or disagreement. This premise has come in the Magnificent Qur'ān in many of its verses, for those with subtle insight and who have opened the ears of their hearts, so that they will receive guidance from Allāh.

Allāh ﷻ says: *And surely you guide (the people) toward the straight path.* Therefore, he ﷺ is a means to gain Divine guidance. Additionally, he ﷺ is even a means in as far as *bay'a* (allegiance) with Allāh is concerned. Allāh says: *Indeed those who took the allegiance with you have taken allegiance with Allāh.*

And Allāh ﷻ says: (*We have revealed the Qur'ān to you*) *that you may explain to the people what has been revealed to them.* So he ﷺ is also a means for us to understand the meaning of the Qur'ān.

Allāh ﷻ further states: *Allāh and His Messenger have more right that they should please Him.* Therefore, his ﷺ pleasure is the means for the one who wants Allāh to have mercy on him and to be pleased with him.

Allāh ﷻ also states:

> *If they come to you, after committing injustice upon*

الفصل العشرون

فِي التَّوَسُّلُ بِهِ صَلَّى اللهُ عَلَيْهِ وَسَلّمَ

وَأَمَّا التَّوَسُّلُ بِهِ صَلَّى اللهُ عَلَيْهِ وَسَلَّمَ فَقَدْ أَجْمَعَ الْعُلَمَاءُ سَلَفاً وَخَلَفاً عَلَى جَوَازِهِ مِنْ غَيْرِ شَكٍّ وَلَا مِرْيَةٍ جَدَلِيَّةٍ ، لِوُرُودِ ذَلِكَ فِي الْقُرْآنِ الْعَظِيمِ فِي آيَاتٍ كَثِيرَةٍ لِمَنْ دَقَّقَ النَّظَرَ وَفَتَحَ مَسَامِعَ قَلْبِهِ فَنَالَ مِنَ اللهِ هُدَاهُ ، كَقَوْلِهِ تَعَالَى : ﴿وَإِنَّكَ لَتَهْدِي إِلَى صِرَاطٍ مُسْتَقِيمٍ ، صِرَاطِ اللهِ﴾ ،

فَهُوَ صَلَّى اللهُ عَلَيْهِ وَسَلَّمَ الْوَسِيلَةُ لِلْهِدَايَةِ الرَّبَّانِيَّةِ ، وَهُوَ صَلَّى اللهُ عَلَيْهِ وَسَلَّمَ الْوَسِيلَةُ فِي الْبَيْعَةِ كَمَا قَالَ تَعَالَى: ﴿إِنَّ الَّذِينَ يُبَايِعُونَكَ إِنَّمَا يُبَايِعُونَ اللهَ﴾ ، وقال تعالى : ﴿لِتُبَيِّنَ لِلنَّاسِ مَا نُزِّلَ إِلَيْهِمْ﴾، فَهُوَ صَلَّى اللهُ عَلَيْهِ وَسَلَّمَ الْوَسِيلَةُ فِي بَيَانِ الْآيَاتِ الرَّبَّانِيَّةِ ،

وَقَالَ تَعَالَى: ﴿وَاللهُ وَرَسُولُهُ أَحَقُّ أَنْ يُرْضُوهُ﴾ فَرِضَاهُ صَلَّى اللهُ عَلَيْهِ وَسَلَّمَ وَسِيلَةٌ لِمَنْ يُرِيدُ أَنْ يَرْحَمَهُ اللهُ وَيَرْضَاهُ ، وَقَوْلِهِ تَعَالَى : ﴿وَلَوْ أَنَّهُمْ إِذْ ظَلَمُوا أَنْفُسَهُمْ جَاءُوكَ فَاسْتَغْفَرُوا اللهَ ، وَاسْتَغْفَرَ لَهُمُ الرَّسُولُ لَوَجَدُوا اللهَ تَوَّاباً رَحِيماً﴾، فَهُوَ

themselves, asking for forgiveness from Allāh, and the Messenger too seeks forgiveness on their behalf, then most certainly they would have found Allāh to be oft-forgiving and most Merciful.

This is because he ﷺ is a means for repentance to be accepted and for Divine mercy to descend. He ﷺ is also a means for the acceptance of one's Islām until the Day of Judgement, since, if someone does not say the second part of the testification of faith: 'that Muḥammad is the Messenger of Allāh', then Allāh will not accept his Islām and the label of disbelief will still be upon him.

Allāh ﷻ again says: *Send salutations upon him and peace in abundance.* Whoever sends blessings on him ﷺ, Allāh sends on that person a Lordly Blessing. He ﷺ is the means for those who send blessings on him ﷺ to obtain the blessing of Allāh. Had it not been for him ﷺ, we would not have been able to acquire this particular blessing from Allāh. And he ﷺ is a means for the all-encompassing mercy to descend on the entire creation, the lofty and the lowly.

Allāh ﷻ has said: *We have not sent you but as a mercy for the worlds.* And even Jibrīl ﷺ has received a portion of this mercy. The Prophet ﷺ is a means for the punishment to be lifted from the creation till the Day of Judgement. Had it not been for him ﷺ, the Earth would have capsized, calamity would have come down, and destructive windstorms would have spread.

Allāh ﷻ states: *And Allāh was not going to punish them while you are in their midst.*

So my brothers! Turn your thoughts to what I and others have written for you, and affirm and be pleased with them. He ﷺ was the means for the descending of serenity to the people who took the pledge at his hands under the tree (*Bay'at al-Riḍwān*). If it was not for him ﷺ, then it would not have taken place and we would

صَلَّى اللهُ عَلَيْهِ وَسَلَّمَ الْوَسِيلَةُ فِى قَبُولِ التَّوْبَةِ ، وَنُزُولِ الرَّحْمَةِ الرَّحْمَانِيَّةِ ، وَهُوَ صَلَّى اللهُ عَلَيْهِ وَسَلَّمَ الْوَسِيلَةُ فِى قَبُولِ الْإِسْلَامِ إِلَى يَوْمِ الْقِيَامَةِ ، إِذْ كُلُّ مَنْ لَمْ يَقُلْ « وَأَنَّ مُحَمَّداً رَسُولُ اللهِ » لَا يَقْبَلُ اللهُ إِسْلَامَهُ وَبِالْكُفْرِ رَمَيْنَاهُ ، وَقَالَ تَعَالَى: ﴿صَلُّوا عَلَيْهِ وَسَلِّمُوا تَسْلِيماً﴾، إِذْ مَنْ صَلَّى عَلَيْهِ صَلَّى اللهُ عَلَيْهِ وَسَلَّمَ، صَلَّى اللهُ عَلَيْهِ صَلَاةً رَبَّانِيَّةً ، فَهُوَ صَلَّى اللهُ عَلَيْهِ وَسَلَّمَ الْوَسِيلَةُ فِى صَلَاةِ اللهِ تَعَالَى عَلَى الْمُصَلِّينَ عَلَى نَبِيِّهِ صَلَّى اللهُ عَلَيْهِ وَسَلَّمَ ، وَلَوْلَاهُ صَلَّى اللهُ عَلَيْهِ وَسَلَّمَ مَا حَصَلَتْ مِنَ اللهِ الصَّلَاةُ ،

وَهُوَ صَلَّى اللهُ عَلَيْهِ وَسَلَّمَ الْوَسِيلَةُ فِى نُزُولِ الرَّحْمَةِ الْعَامَّةِ إِلَى سَائِرِ الْخَلَائِقِ الْعُلْوِيَّةِ وَالسُّفْلِيَّةِ ، قَالَ تَعَالَى: ﴿وَمَا أَرْسَلْنَاكَ إِلَّا رَحْمَةً لِلْعَالَمِينَ﴾، وَقَدْ نَالَ شَيْئاً مِنْ هَذِهِ الرَّحْمَةِ جِبْرِيلُ عَلَيْهِ سَلَامُ اللهُ ، وَهُوَ صَلَّى اللهُ عَلَيْهِ وَسَلَّمَ الْوَسِيلَةُ فِى رَفْعِ الْعَذَابِ عَنِ الْخَلْقِ إِلَى يَوْمِ الْقِيَامَةِ ، وَلَوْلَاهُ صَلَّى اللهُ عَلَيْهِ وَسَلَّمَ لَقُلِبَتِ الْأَرْضُ وَنَزَلَ الْحَاصِبُ ، وَجَاءَتِ الرِّيَاحُ الْمُهْلِكَةُ الذَّرِّيَّةُ ، قَالَ تَعَالَى: ﴿وَمَا كَانَ اللهُ لِيُعَذِّبَهُمْ وَأَنْتَ فِيهِمْ﴾ فَجُلْ بِفِكْرِكَ يَا أَخَانَا فِيمَا كَتَبْتُهُ لَكَ وَغَيْرِى أَقَرَّهُ وَارْتَضَاهُ ،

وَهُوَ الْوَسِيلَةُ صَلَّى اللهُ عَلَيْهِ وَسَلَّمَ فِى نُزُولِ السَّكِينَةِ عَلَى أَهْلِ بَيْعَةِ الشَّجَرَةِ الرِّضْوَانِيَّةِ ، إِذْ لَوْلَاهُ صَلَّى اللهُ عَلَيْهِ وَسَلَّمَ مَا كَانَ ذَلِكَ وَلَا سَمِعْنَاهُ ، وَمِنَ السُّنَّةِ

not have even heard about it. It is mentioned in the ḥadith of the blind man of which there is no doubt, suspicion, or concern, and has been reported with acceptance by al-Ḥāfiẓ al-Mundhirī ؓ and others. Regarding *tawassul*, which is to seek him ﷺ as a means in one's supplication to the Lord of creation, it is commendable and desirable, during his lifetime and after it.

Allāh ﷻ says: *They (the prophets) enjoy many ranks by Allāh* If it were not for these ranks, Allāh would not accept the supplication of the supplicant when he calls Him. Have the ranks of the Prophet ﷺ decreased after his passing? Whosoever believes that has disbelieved, with the disbelief of idolatry. Nay, he ﷺ is alive with Allāh, with a life that is much better than the first life (that he had on this Earth). This fact is known to all those who are devoted to him ﷺ. *Amīr al-Mu'minīn*, Sayyiduna 'Umar ؓ said (whilst making du'ā for rain): "*O Allāh we used to supplicate to You, making Your Prophet as a means.*"

Meaning, we would seek rain from You, through means of Your Prophet ﷺ due to his lofty position and sublime status with You. When his prayer for rain ceased (after his ﷺ physical death), his uncle 'Abbās ؓ was brought forth, and 'Umar ؓ would seek a means with the Prophet ﷺ through his close relations and say, "because of his close family ties with Your Prophet ﷺ." Therefore, ponder and take heed of my statement and do not follow those who have deviated and follow their base desires.

[Imām] Ibn Taymiyya ؓ has narrated that the pious predecessors used to supplicate with the method of the ḥadith of the blind man. Imām Aḥmad ؓ commanded his student al-Marwazī ؓ to supplicate using as a means the best of creation ﷺ. Our shaykh, [Shaykh] al-Shinqīṭi ؓ, has said that this statement above is authentic without any doubt and confusion. Furthermore, the ḥadith stat-

حَدِيثُ الْأَعْمَى مِنْ غَيْرِ شَكٍّ وَلَا رِيبَةٍ وَهْمِيَّةٍ ، الَّذِى ارْتَضَاهُ الْحُفَّاظُ كَالْحَافِظِ الْمُنْذِرِيِّ وَمَنْ وَالَاهُ ، وَأَمَّا التَّوَسُّلُ بِهِ صَلَّى اللهُ عَلَيْهِ وَسَلَّمَ فَمُسْتَحَبٌّ وَمُرَغَّبٌ فِيهِ فِى الدَّعَوَاتِ لِرَبِّ الْبَرِيَّةِ ، فِى الْحَيَاةِ وَبَعْدَهَا ، لِقَوْلِهِ تَعَالَى: ﴿هُمْ دَرَجَاتٌ عِنْدَ اللهِ﴾ فَلَوْلَا الدَّرَجَاتُ لَمَا قَبِلَ اللهُ دُعَاءَ دَاعٍ دَعَاهُ ،

وَهَلِ النَّبِيُّ صَلَّى اللهُ عَلَيْهِ وَسَلَّمَ بَعْدَ وَفَاتِهِ نَقَصَتْ دَرَجَاتُهُ ؟ فَمَنْ اعْتَقَدَ ذَلِكَ فَقَدْ كَفَرَ كُفْرَ الْوَثَنِيَّةِ ، بَلْ هُوَ صَلَّى اللهُ عَلَيْهِ وَسَلَّمَ حَيٌّ عِنْدَ اللهِ تَعَالَى بِحَيَاةٍ تَفْضُلُ الْحَيَاةَ الْأُولَى ، عِنْدَ كُلِّ مَنْ عَرَفَ ذَلِكَ وَوَعَاهُ ، وَقَدْ قَالَ أَمِيرُ الْمُؤْمِنِينَ سَيِّدُنَا عُمَرُ رَضِىَ اللهُ عَنْهُ: «اللَّهُمَّ إِنَّا كُنَّا نَتَوَسَّلُ إِلَيْكَ بِنَبِيِّكَ صَلَّى اللهُ عَلَيْهِ وَسَلَّمَ »

فَمَعْنَاهُ كُنَّا نَسْتَسْقِى بِهِ مُتَوَسِّلِينَ بِهِ إِلَيْكَ بِدَرَجَاتِهِ عِنْدَكَ وَمَنْزِلَتِهِ الْعَلِيَّةِ ، وَلَمَّا امْتَنَعَتْ صَلَاتُهُ صَلَّى اللهُ عَلَيْهِ وَسَلَّمَ فِى الاسْتِسْقَاءِ قَدَّمَ عَمَّهُ الْعَبَّاسَ لِلصَّلَاةِ ، وَتَوَسَّلَ بِالنَّبِيِّ صَلَّى اللهُ عَلَيْهِ وَسَلَّمَ فِى قَرَابَتِهِ فَقَالَ : « لِقَرَابَتِهِ مِنْ نَبِيِّكَ صَلَّى اللهُ عَلَيْهِ وَسَلَّمَ » ، فَفَكِّرْ فِى هَذَا وَلَا تَتَّبِعْ مَنْ اتَّبَعَ غَيَّهُ وَهَوَاهُ ،

وَنَقَلَ ابْنُ تَيْمِيَةَ أَنَّ السَّلَفَ الصَّالِحَ كَانُوا يَدْعُونَ بِحَدِيثِ الْأَعْمَى ، وَأَنَّ الْإِمَامَ أَحْمَدَ رَضِىَ اللهُ عَنْهُ أَمَرَ تِلْمِيذَهُ الْمَرْوَزِىَّ فِى مَنْسَكٍ لَهُ أَنْ يَتَوَسَّلَ بِخَيْرِ الْبَرِيَّةِ ، قَالَ شَيْخُنَا الشَّنْقِيطِىُّ رَحِمَهُ اللهُ : « وَهَذَا نَقْلٌ صَحِيحٌ مِنْ غَيْرِ شَكٍّ

ing that Ādam ﷺ sought the means of the Prophet ﷺ is mentioned by [Imām] al-Ḥākim ﷺ in his *Mustadrak*, with an authentic chain of narration. This information is from what Shaykh al-Nabhānī ﷺ has compiled in his books. The same thing has been narrated by Ibn al-Ḥajj al-Mālikī ﷺ and it has been agreed upon by the scholars of al-Azhar and the Shaykh of the *Maliki* masters. I have found that all of the scholars of al-Azhar seek a means to Allāh through the Messenger of Allāh ﷺ.

From what indicates to seeking means through him ﷺ is the ḥadith of intercession on the Day of Judgement for the entirety of mankind. As has been recorded by Imām al-Bukhari ﷺ and others. How magnificent is the status and rank of this Prophet ﷺ and how sublime is he!

> "O Allāh we turn to You by means of your Prophet, our Master Muḥammad, the Prophet of mercy and beneficence."
>
> "O our Master, O Muḥammad, O Messenger of Allāh (x3), we are turning by means of you to our Lord, that He fulfil our needs and grants us what we supplicate for and what we desire."
>
> "O Allāh allow him to intercede on our behalf, such an intercession that is accepted and You are pleased with, and that we have the benefit of that intercession in our lives and after our death, wherever we are by the benevolence of Allāh."
>
> "O Messenger of Allāh, intercede for us as your intercession is accepted. And your status with Allah no doubt benefits."

وَلَا اشْتِبَاهٍ» ، وَحَدِيثُ تَوَسُّلِ آدَمَ بِهِ عَلَيْهِ الصَّلَاةُ وَالسَّلَامُ أَخْرَجَهُ الْحَاكِمُ فِي الْمُسْتَدْرَكِ بِالْأَحَادِيثِ الصَّحِيحَةِ الْمَرْوِيَّةِ ، وَغَيْرُ ذَلِكَ مِمَّا جَمَعَهُ الشَّيْخُ النَّبَهَانِيُّ فِي كُتُبِهِ وَجَمَعَهُ وَوَفَّاهُ ، وَالَّذِى نَقَلَهُ ابْنُ الْحَاجِّ الْمَالِكِيُّ فِي الْمَدْخَلِ ، وَوَافَقَهُ عَلَيْهِ عُلَمَاءُ الْأَزْهَرِ ، وَشَيْخُ السَّادَةِ الْمَالِكِيَّةِ ، وَقَدْ أَدْرَكْتُ جَمِيعَ عُلَمَاءُ الْأَزْهَرِ يَتَوَسَّلُونَ بِرَسُولِ اللهِ ،

وَمِمَّا يَدُلُّ عَلَى التَّوَسُّلِ بِهِ صَلَّى اللهُ عَلَيْهِ وَسَلَّمَ حَدِيثُ الشَّفَاعَةِ يَوْمَ الْقِيَامَةِ مِنْ جَمِيعِ الْأُمَمِ الْإِنْسَانِيَّةِ ، كَمَا أَخْرَجَهُ الْإِمَامُ الْبُخَارِيُّ وَغَيْرُهُ ، فَمَا أَعْظَمَ قَدْرَ هَذَا النَّبِيِّ صَلَّى اللهُ عَلَيْهِ وَسَلَّمَ وَأَعْلَاهُ ،

اللّٰهُمَّ إِنَّا نَتَوَجَّهُ إِلَيْكَ بِنَبِيِّكَ سَيِّدِنَا مُحَمَّدٍ نَبِيِّ الرَّحْمَةِ الرَّحْمَانِيَّةِ ، يَا سَيِّدَنَا يَا مُحَمَّدُ يَا رَسُولَ اللهِ (ثَلَاثَ مَرَّاتٍ) إِنَّا نَتَوَجَّهُ بِكَ إِلَى رَبِّنَا فِي أَنْ يَقْضِيَ حَوَائِجَنَا وَمَا دَعَوْنَا بِهِ وَمَا قَصَدْنَاهُ ، اللّٰهُمَّ شَفِّعْهُ فِينَا شَفَاعَةً مَقْبُولَةً مَرْضِيَّةً ، يُدْرِكُنَا نَفْعُهَا فِي حَيَاتِنَا وَمَمَاتِنَا حَيْثُ مَا كُنَّا بِفَضْلِ اللهِ ،

تَشَفَّعْ رَسُولَ اللهِ أَنْتَ مُشَفَّعُ   وَجَاهُكَ عِنْدَ اللهِ لَا شَكَّ يَنْفَعُ

O Allāh send blessings, peace and abundance on our liege and master, Muḥammad, the best of creation, and on his family, in every glance and breath, as many times as all that is contained in the knowledge of Allāh.

﴿اللَّهُمَّ صَلِّ وَسَلِّمْ وَبَارِكْ عَلَى سَيِّدِنَا وَمَوْلَانَا مُحَمَّدٍ خَيْرِ الْبَرِيَّةِ،
وَعَلَى آلِهِ فِي كُلِّ لَمْحَةٍ وَنَفَسٍ عَدَدَ مَا وَسِعَهُ عِلْمُ اللهِ﴾

CHAPTER 21

Regarding the Life of Rasul Allāh ﷺ after His Departure from this World

As for the Prophet's life after death, the masters of ḥadith and the scholars have established it by using the verse of the Qur'ān regarding the life of the martyrs. They have said that his being alive is established by the principle of being more deserving [to have this honor]. The scholars of Shinqīṭ have said, "Rather, his life ﷺ is loftier than the life of the martyrs. As such, it is allowed to marry the wives (widows) of the martyr but it is forbidden for the believing men to marry the wives of Prophet ﷺ. That itself is due to his intense protective jealousy, and the fact that he ﷺ is in a sublime elevated state, aware and alive." As for his wives, there was no waiting period for them nor is his wealth inherited. That indicates the perfection of his life. This is attested by the scholars of the *Shinqīṭiyya* ﷺ. Know [this]! His honorable body ﷺ does not decay, rather, it remains preserved.

[Imām] al-Zurqānī ﷺ, has narrated in his commentary of the *Muwaṭṭa'* of Imām Malik ﷺ, in the chapter regarding the qualities of Sayyiduna 'Isā, upon our Prophet and him be the blessings of Allāh, that the scholars have said as commentary of his statement ﷺ: *There is not anyone who greets me except that Allāh returns my soul to me and I return the greeting.*

الفصل الحادى والعشرون

فِى حَيَاتِهِ صَلَّى اللهُ عَلَيْهِ وَسَلَّمَ بَعْدَ الْمَوْتِ

وأَمَّا حَيَاتِهِ صَلَّى اللهُ عَلَيْهِ وَسَلَّمَ بَعْدَ الْمَوْتِ فَقَدْ أَثْبَتَهَا الْحُفَّاظُ وَالْعُلَمَاءُ بِآيَةِ حَيَاةِ الشُّهَدَاءِ، وَقَالُوا : حَيَاتُهُ صَلَّى اللهُ عَلَيْهِ وَسَلَّمَ ثَابِتَةٌ بِالْأَوْلَوِيَّةِ ، وَقَالَ عُلَمَاءُ شَنْقِيطَ رَحِمَهُمُ اللهُ : بَلْ حَيَاتُهُ صَلَّى اللهُ عَلَيْهِ وَسَلَّمَ أَرْقَى مِنْ حَيَاةِ الشُّهَدَاءِ، حَيْثُ أَبَاحَ اللهُ تَعَالَى تَزْوِيجَ نِسَائِهِمْ وَحَرَّمَ عَلَى الْمُؤْمِنِينَ تَزَوُّجَ نِسَائِهِ صَلَّى اللهُ عَلَيْهِ وَسَلَّمَ ، وَذَلِكَ لِشِدَّةِ غَيْرَتِهِ صَلَّى اللهُ عَلَيْهِ وَسَلَّمَ ، وَأَنَّهُ فِى رُقِيٍّ سَامٍ وَإِدْرَاكٍ وَحَيَاةٍ ، وَلَا عِدَّةَ عَلَى نِسَائِهِ رَضِىَ اللهُ عَنْهُنَّ ، وَلَا يُورَثُ مَالُهُ وَذَلِكَ يَدُلُّ عَلَى كَمَالِ الْحَيَاةِ ، كَمَا قَرَّرَ ذَلِكَ عُلَمَاءُ الدِّيَارِ الشَّنْقِيطِيَّةِ ،

وَاعْلَمْ أَنَّ جَسَدَهُ صَلَّى اللهُ عَلَيْهِ وَسَلَّمَ لاَ يَبْلَى ، بَلْ هُوَ بَاقٍ مَحْفُوظٌ ،وَنَقَلَ الزُّرْقَانِيُّ رَحِمَهُ اللهُ فِى شَرْحِهِ لِمُوَطَّإِ الْإِمَامِ مَالِكٍ رَضِىَ اللهُ عَنْهُ فِى بَابِ صِفَةِ الْمَسِيحِ عِيسَى ابْنِ مَرْيَمَ عَلَى نَبِيِّنَا وَعَلَيْهِ صَلَوَاتُ اللهِ ، أَنَّ الْعُلَمَاءَ قَالُوا فِى شَرْحِ حَدِيثِهِ صَلَّى اللهُ عَلَيْهِ وَسَلَّمَ: « مَا مِنْ أَحَدٍ يُسَلِّمُ عَلَيَّ إِلَّا رَدَّ اللهُ عَلَيَّ رُوحِى فَأَرُدَّ عَلَيْهِ السَّلَامَ » أَنَّ أَوَّلَ وَاحِدٍ مِنْ أُمَّتِهِ يُسَلِّمُ عَلَيْهِ بَعْدَ دَفْنِهِ بِقَبْرِهِ

'So [from] the first person who greeted him ﷺ from his nation after he was placed in his grave, Allāh returned his soul to him and it will remain in his body till the day of witnessing the conditions of the Hereafter. And this is a pure and authentic statement which corresponds with reality, and how pleasant and sweet it is.'

The Glorious Qurʾān indicates that the bodies of the prophets ﷺ are preserved after death. In the story of Sulaymān ﷺ, it states that he stood resting upon his staff for the entire year. If it were anyone else, then they would have broken into pieces and their appearance would have changed. The Prophet ﷺ said, as narrated in the Sunan of al-Tirmidhī: "Indeed Allāh has forbidden the Earth to devour the bodies of the prophets." Allāh informed the Prophet ﷺ that He will send salutations upon him.

Verily, Allāh and His angels shower blessings on the Prophet. O Believers! Send blessings upon him and salute him with a worthy salutation.

The word "*yuṣallū*" is used in the verse; according to the science of Arabic grammar, it is in the present continuous form which indicates the constant renewal of the state. Allāh ﷻ commanded the believers also to send blessings and peace upon him ﷺ till the end of time. And does Allāh, His angels and the believers send blessings on other than a Prophet, [who has] body, soul, and a pure established life? Listen well to these words of mine! O one whom Allāh has opened the ears of his heart to the maʿrifa (knowledge) of His Prophet ﷺ, and guided him, and showed him the way! How can it not be like this, when he is *al-Sirāj al-Munīr* (the Illuminating Lamp), through which the other lamps, who previously were without light, take their light from! And he ﷺ is like the sun, which is one, but can be seen all over the world without doubt or confusion.

الشَّرِيفِ يَرُدُّ اللهُ عَلَيْهِ رُوحَهُ ، فَتَبْقَى فِي جَسَدِهِ إِلَى يَوْمِ مُشَاهَدَةِ الْأَحْوَالِ الْأُخْرَوِيَّةِ ، وَذَلِكَ كَلَامٌ طَيِّبٌ صَحِيحٌ ، مُطَابِقٌ لِلْوَاقِعِ ، فَمَا أَعْذَبَهُ وَمَا أَحْلَاهُ ،

وَقَدْ دَلَّ الْقُرْآنُ الْعَظِيمُ عَلَى حِفْظِ أَجْسَامِ الْأَنْبِيَاءِ بَعْدَ الْمَوْتِ فِي قِصَّةِ سُلَيْمَانَ عَلَيْهِ السَّلَامُ الْمَرْوِيَّةِ ، وَهُوَ أَنَّهُ قَدْ مَكَثَ سَنَةً مُتَّكِئاً عَلَى عَصًا ، فَلَوْ كَانَ عَلَيْهِ السَّلَامُ كَغَيْرِهِ لَتَحَطَّمَ وَتَغَيَّرَ مَرْآهُ ، وَقَالَ عَلَيْهِ الصَّلَاةُ وَالسَّلَامُ : « إِنَّ اللهَ حَرَّمَ عَلَى الْأَرْضِ أَنْ تَأْكُلَ أَجْسَادَ الْأَنْبِيَاءِ » ، رِوَايَةً فِي السُّنَنِ التِّرْمِذِيَّةِ ، وَقَدْ أَخْبَرَ اللهُ تَعَالَى أَنَّهُ يُصَلِّي عَلَيْهِ ، وَذَلِكَ بِالْفِعْلِ الْمُضَارِعِ الَّذِي يَدُلُّ عَلَى تَجَدُّدِ الْحَدَثِ عِنْدَ أَهْلِ الْعُلُومِ النَّحْوِيَّةِ . وَأَمَرَ بِالصَّلَاةِ وَالسَّلَامِ عَلَيْهِ إِلَى آخِرِ الزَّمَانِ وَمُنْتَهَاهُ ، وَهَلْ يُصَلِّي اللهُ تَعَالَى وَمَلَائِكَتُهُ وَالْمُؤْمِنُونَ إِلَّا عَلَى نَبِيٍّ بِجِسْمِهِ وَرُوحِهِ وَحَيَاةٍ ثَابِتَةٍ زَكِيَّةٍ ، فَاسْمَعْ كَلَامِي هَذَا يَا مَنْ فَتَحَ اللهُ مَسَامِعَ قَلْبِهِ إِلَى مَعْرِفَةِ نَبِيِّهِ صَلَّى اللهُ عَلَيْهِ وَسَلَّمَ وَأَرْشَدَهُ وَدَلَّاهُ ،

وَكَيْفَ لَا يَكُونُ كَذَلِكَ وَهُوَ صَلَّى اللهُ عَلَيْهِ وَسَلَّمَ السِّرَاجُ الْمُنِيرُ الَّذِي مِنْهُ تَتَّقِدُ السُّرُجُ الْمُطْفِيَّةُ ، وَهُوَ صَلَّى اللهُ عَلَيْهِ وَسَلَّمَ كَالشَّمْسِ فَإِنَّهَا وَاحِدَةٌ وَلَكِنَّهَا تُرَى فِي جَمِيعِ الْبِقَاعِ بِلَا شَكٍّ وَلَا اشْتِبَاهٍ ، وَقَدْ وَرَدَ فِي السُّنَّةِ الصَّحِيحَةِ حُضُورُ الْأَنْبِيَاءِ عَلَيْهِمُ الصَّلَاةُ وَالسَّلَامُ فِي لَيْلَةِ الْإِسْرَاءِ وَانْتِقَالُهُمْ مِنْ قُبُورِهِمْ إِلَى بَيْتِ الْمَقْدِسِ إِلَى السَّمَوَاتِ الْعُلْوِيَّةِ ، وَرَأَى النَّبِيُّ صَلَّى اللهُ عَلَيْهِ وَسَلَّمَ سَيِّدَنَا مُوسَى

It is reported in the authentic sunna that the prophets عليهم السلام were present on the night of the Isrāʾ, having been transported from their respective graves to Bayt al-Maqdis, then to the heavens. The Prophet ﷺ saw Sayyiduna Mūsā عليه السلام standing and praying in his grave. He also saw him coming down into the valleys of Makka responding [with *talbiya*] to his Creator and Patron عز وجل.

The scholars are unanimous that whatever is established for the prophets عليهم السلام, in terms of miracles after their deaths, applies a fortiori for our Prophet ﷺ.

The Prophet ﷺ saw the [other] Prophets عليهم السلام in a wakeful state after their passing; therefore it is possible to likewise see him ﷺ. And many of the pious have informed [us] about the witnessing and vision of him ﷺ while awake.

Imām al-Bukhari رحمه الله has mentioned that the Prophet ﷺ said: "He who has seen me in his dreams, will see me while awake," meaning in this world, in a state of wakefulness, as has been related by Imām al-Suyūṭī رحمه الله and other scholars of the 'accepted sect' (*Ahl al-Sunna wa al-Jamāʿa*). It has also been narrated that the salutations sent to him ﷺ, reach him ﷺ, regardless of how remote or how far the place is.

So, O my brothers in Allāh, do not be heedless about what I have indicated to you of these experiential allusions and gems, which I have pointed out to you from what has been corroborated by authentic and strong chains of narration. May it be that you are favored, by presenting your soul at the remembrance of his *Mawlid* ﷺ with spiritual witnessing, which is the objective of the ardent lovers, the shimmering flashes of the beauty of his light and splendor ﷺ.

عَلَيْهِ السَّلَامُ قَائِمًا عِنْدَ قَبْرِهِ يُصَلِّي ، وَهَابِطاً بِمَكَّةَ مِنَ الْوَادِي يُلَبِّي خَالِقَهُ وَمَوْلَاهُ ، وَقَدْ أَجْمَعَ الْعُلَمَاءُ عَلَى أَنَّ مَا ثَبَتَ لِلْأَنْبِيَاءِ عَلَيْهِمُ الصَّلَاةُ وَالسَّلَامُ مِنْ مُعْجِزَاتٍ بَعْدَ مَمَاتِهِمْ فَهِيَ ثَابِتَةٌ لِنَبِيِّنَا صَلَّى اللهُ عَلَيْهِ وَسَلَّمَ بِطَرِيقِ الْأَوْلَوِيَّةِ ،

وَقَدْ رَأَى صَلَّى اللهُ عَلَيْهِ وَسَلَّمَ الْأَنْبِيَاءَ عَلَيْهِمُ الصَّلَاةُ وَالسَّلَامُ يَقَظَةً بَعْدَ الْمَوْتِ ، فَتَجُوزُ رُؤْيَتُهُ صَلَّى اللهُ عَلَيْهِ وَسَلَّمَ كَذَلِكَ ، وَكَثِيرٌ مِنَ الصَّالِحِينَ قَدْ أَخْبَرَ أَنَّهُ فِي حَالِ الْيَقَظَةِ قَدْ شَاهَدَهُ وَرَآهُ ،

وَأَخْرَجَ الْبُخَارِيُّ عَنْهُ صَلَّى اللهُ عَلَيْهِ وَسَلَّمَ أَنَّهُ قَالَ: « مَنْ رَآنِي فِي النَّوْمِ فَسَيَرَانِي فِي الْيَقَظَةِ » ، أَيْ فِي الدُّنْيَا، يَقَظَةً ، كَمَا نَقَلَ ذَلِكَ السُّيُوطِيُّ وَغَيْرُهُ مِنْ عُلَمَاءِ الْمِلَّةِ الْمَرْضِيَّةِ ، وَقَدْ وَرَدَ أَيْضًا أَنَّ سَلَامَ الْمُسَلِّمِ عَلَيْهِ يَبْلُغُهُ صَلَّى اللهُ عَلَيْهِ وَسَلَّمَ مِنْ أَبْعَدِ بَلَدٍ وَأَقْصَاهُ ،

فَلَا تَكُنْ غَافِلاً يَا أَخَانَا فِي اللهِ تَعَالَى عَمَّا أَشَرْتُ بِهِ إِلَيْكَ مِنَ الْإِشَارَاتِ الذَّوْقِيَّةِ، مِمَّا أَشَرْتُ بِهِ إِلَيْكَ مِنْ دُرَرِ الْقَوْلِ الْمُدَلَّلِ بِصَحِيحِ السَّنَدِ وَأَقْوَاهُ، فَلَعَلَّكَ أَنْ تَحْظَى بِشُهُودِ رُوحِكَ عِنْدَ ذِكْرِ مَوْلِدِهِ صَلَّى اللهُ عَلَيْهِ وَسَلَّمَ بِالْمُشَاهَدَةِ الْقَلْبِيَّةِ الَّتِي هِيَ غَايَةُ الْمُتَشَوِّقِينَ إِلَى لَمَحَاتِ لَمَعَانِ جَمَالِ نُورِهِ صَلَّى اللهُ عَلَيْهِ وَسَلَّمَ وَسَنَاهُ ،

O Allāh send blessings, peace and abundance on our liege and master, Muḥammad, the best of creation, and on his family, in every glance and breath, as many times as all that is contained in the knowledge of Allāh.

﴿اللّٰهُمَّ صَلِّ وَسَلِّمْ وَبَارِكْ عَلَى سَيِّدِنَا وَمَوْلَانَا مُحَمَّدٍ خَيْرِ الْبَرِيَّةِ،
وَعَلَى آلِهِ فِي كُلِّ لَمْحَةٍ وَنَفَسٍ عَدَدَ مَا وَسِعَهُ عِلْمُ اللّٰهِ﴾

CHAPTER 22

Concerning some of His ﷺ Miracles (Muʿjizāt)

As for the miracles of the Prophet ﷺ, these are numerous, well-known, and well-documented. The Ṣaḥāba have narrated these incidents and witnessed them with their very eyes.

From among the miracles:

1. There was a rock in Makka which used to greet him ﷺ by saying: Peace be upon you O Messenger of Allāh"

2. The disbelievers of Makka demanded that he ﷺ split the moon. So, he ﷺ split the moon into two pieces. This scene was witnessed by a group of the disbelievers and he ﷺ said to them, "Bear witness! Bear witness!" The disbelievers however, said, "Muḥammad has bewitched the moon." This has been narrated by Imām al-Bukhari

3. The lizard speaking to him ﷺ in clear Arabic

4. A camel complained and prostrated to him ﷺ. He heard its grievance and complaint

الفصل الثانى والعشرون

فِي بَعْضِ مُعْجِزَاتِهِ صَلَّى اللّٰهُ عَلَيْهِ وَسَلَّمَ

وَأَمَّا مُعْجِزَاتِهِ صَلَّى اللّٰهُ عَلَيْهِ وَسَلَّمَ فَكَثِيرَةٌ مَشْهُورَةٌ نَقَلَهَا أَصْحَابُهُ رَضِىَ اللّٰهُ عَنْهُمْ وَرَأَوْهَا بِالْأَعْيُنِ الْبَصَرِيَّةِ ، مِنْهَا:

١. أَنَّ حَجَراً بِمَكَّةَ كَانَ يُسَلِّمُ عَلَيْهِ صَلَّى اللّٰهُ عَلَيْهِ وَسَلَّمَ يَقُولُ: السَّلَامُ عَلَيْكَ يَا رَسُولَ اللّٰهِ ،

٢. وَقَدْ طَلَبَ الْمُشْرِكُونَ مِنْهُ صَلَّى اللّٰهُ عَلَيْهِ وَسَلَّمَ انْشِقَاقَ الْقَمَرِ فَانْشَقَّ فِرْقَتَيْنِ ، وَقَدْ شَاهَدَتِ الْفِئَةُ الْكُفْرِيَّةُ ، فَقَالَ صَلَّى اللّٰهُ عَلَيْهِ وَسَلَّمَ: اشْهَدُوا ، اشْهَدُوا ، فَقَالَ الْكُفَّارُ سَحَرَ مُحَمَّدٌ الْقَمَرِ!! نَقَلَ ذَلِكَ الْبُخَارِيُّ

٣. وَرَوَاهُ ، وَكَلَامُ الضَبِّ مَعَهُ صَلَّى اللّٰهُ عَلَيْهِ وَسَلَّمَ بِاللُّغَةِ الْعَرَبِيَّةِ ،

٤. وَشَكْوَى الْبَعِيرِ وَسُجُودُهُ لَهُ صَلَّى اللّٰهُ عَلَيْهِ وَسَلَّمَ ، وَقَدْ سَمِعَ صَلَّى اللّٰهُ عَلَيْهِ وَسَلَّمَ تَظَلُّمَهُ وَشَكْوَاهُ ،

5. A pure and wholesome stream of water gushed forth from his ﷺ fingers and the army of the Muhājirūn and a group of the Anṣār quenched their thirst from it

6. When he ﷺ mixed his blessed saliva to the food of Jābir ﷺ, which was one *Saa'* of barley (3.25 kg) and a young she-goat, Allāh put blessings of abundance in it so that the entire army was satiated by it, while the original quantity still remained as if untouched. This was narrated by Jābir b. 'Abd Allāh ﷺ himself

7. He ﷺ once summoned some trees, and they uprooted themselves, came to him, and covered him, as though they were a built-up room

8. Clouds provided their shade to him ﷺ and protected him from the heat whenever he was on a journey or walking

9. The lofty mountains tried to entice him by turning themselves into mountains of gold. And the earthly treasures were presented to him ﷺ, but he adopted abstinence and turned away from them. So, Allāh expanded his chest and enriched him ﷺ

10. The trunk of a date palm tree cried and wept affectionately, craving and yearning for him ﷺ, during his *Jumu'a* sermons

11. When one of the eyes of Qatāda ﷺ protruded out from its place and he ﷺ pushed it back in, his eyesight was

٥. وَقَدْ نَبَعَ الْمَاءُ مِنْ بَيْنِ أَصَابِعِهِ صَلَّى اللهُ عَلَيْهِ وَسَلَّمَ فَأَرْوَى جَيْشَ الْمُهَاجِرِينَ وَالْفِئَةِ الْأَنْصَارِيَّةِ ،

٦. وَلَمَّا بَصَقَ صَلَّى اللهُ عَلَيْهِ وَسَلَّمَ فِي طَعَامِ جَابِرٍ وَهُوَ صَاعٌ مِنْ شَعِيرٍ وَعَنَاقٌ صَغِيرَةٌ بَارَكَ اللهُ تَعَالَى فِيهِ فَشَبِعَ الْجَيْشُ ، وَبَقِيَ الطَّعَامُ كَمَا هُوَ ، حَكَى ذَلِكَ جَابِرُ بْنُ عَبْدِ اللهِ ،

٧. وَدَعَا صَلَّى اللهُ عَلَيْهِ وَسَلَّمَ الْأَشْجَارَ فَجَاءَتْ إِلَيْهِ وَسَتَرَتْهُ كَأَنَّهَا حُجْرَةٌ مَبْنِيَّةٌ ،

٨. وَظَلَّلَتْهُ صَلَّى اللهُ عَلَيْهِ وَسَلَّمَ الْغَمَامَةُ فِي الْحَرِّ وَهِيَ تَتْبَعُهُ فِي سَيْرِهِ وَمَمْشَاهُ ،

٩. وَرَاوَدَتْهُ الْجِبَالُ الشُّمُّ أَنْ تَكُونَ لَهُ ذَهَباً ، وَعُرِضَتْ عَلَيْهِ صَلَّى اللهُ عَلَيْهِ وَسَلَّمَ الْكُنُوزُ الْأَرْضِيَّةُ ، فَزَهِدَ فِيهَا صَلَّى اللهُ عَلَيْهِ وَسَلَّمَ وَأَعْرَضَ عَنْهَا فَشَرَحَ اللهُ صَدْرَهُ وَأَغْنَاهُ ،

١٠. وَالْجِذْعُ حَنَّ لَهُ صَلَّى اللهُ عَلَيْهِ وَسَلَّمَ ، شَوْقاً إِلَى خُطَبِهِ الْجُمُعِيَّةِ ،

١١. وَرَدَّ صَلَّى اللهُ عَلَيْهِ وَسَلَّمَ عَيْنَ قَتَادَةَ فَعَادَتْ أَحْسَنَ مِمَّا كَانَتْ ، وَإِذَا رَمِدَتِ الْعَيْنُ الْأُخْرَى صَرَفَ اللهُ تَعَالَى عَنْهَا الرَّمَدَ

better than it was originally. When the other eye got inflamed, Allāh removed the inflammation and granted it relief as well

12. When Ibn ʿAfrāʾ ؓ injured his arm, it was healed by the blessing of the saliva of the Prophet ﷺ. It is a remedy for all physical and spiritual ailments

13. He ﷺ gave a date palm branch to ʿUkkāsha ؓ which turned into an unsheathed, shining sword, vibrating in his hands

14. He ﷺ applied his blessed saliva onto the infected eyes of Sayyiduna ʿAlī, may Allāh ennoble his countenance, and through the '*Muḥammadan Baraka*' the ailment was cured

15. A wolf informed the shepherd about his advent ﷺ and even directed the shepherd to him ﷺ

16. [Shaykh] al-Ḍumayrī ؒ mentioned in his book under the letter *Ẓā* (ظ), that a gazelle spoke to him ﷺ. He mentions numerous chains for this narration

17. He ﷺ blessed Abū Hurayra ؓ with a bag of dates, which remained with him for years but were not depleted

18. He ﷺ put his blessed saliva into salty water, after which the water became sweet like the water of the Nile

19. He ﷺ offered a bowl of milk to the Ahl al-Ṣuffa ؓ, who were more than seventy in number, and all of them were

١٢. وَأَذَاهُ ، وَرَدَّ ذِرَاعَ ابْنِ عَفْرَاءَ فَعَادَ سَلِيماً بِبَرَكَةِ رِيقِهِ صَلَّى اللهُ عَلَيْهِ وَسَلَّمَ الَّذِى هُوَ دَوَاءٌ مِنَ الْعِلَلِ الْحِسِّيَّةِ وَالْمَعْنَوِيَّةِ ،

١٣. وَأَعْطَى صَلَّى اللهُ عَلَيْهِ وَسَلَّمَ لِعُكَّاشَةَ رَضِىَ اللهُ عَنْهُ عُرْجُوناً ، فَعَادَ سَيْفاً صَلْتاً يَهْتَزُّ فِى يُمْنَاهُ ،

١٤. وَتَفَلَ فِى عَيْنَىْ سَيِّدِنَا عَلِيٍّ رَضِىَ اللهُ عَنْهُ وَكَرَّمَ اللهُ وَجْهَهُ ، فَذَهَبَ الرَّمَدُ وَشَفَاهُ اللهُ تَعَالَى بِالْبَرَكَةِ الْمُحَمَّدِيَّةِ ،

١٥. وَأَخْبَرَ الذِّئْبُ الرَّاعِىَ بِظُهُورِهِ صَلَّى اللهُ عَلَيْهِ وَسَلَّمَ ، وَدَلَّهُ عَلَيْهِ وَهَدَاهُ ،

١٦. وَحَكَى الدُّمَيْرِىُّ فِى حَرْفِ الظَّاءِ أَنَّ الْغَزَالَةَ خَاطَبَتْهُ صَلَّى اللهُ عَلَيْهِ وَسَلَّمَ ، وَذَكَرَ الْحَدِيثَ بِطُرُقٍ مَرْوِيَّةٍ ،

١٧. وَبَارَكَ صَلَّى اللهُ عَلَيْهِ وَسَلَّمَ لِأَبِى هُرَيْرَةَ جِرَابَ تَمْرٍ ، فَمَكَثَ سِنِينَ يَأْكُلُ مِنْهُ وَمَا أَفْنَاهُ ،

١٨. وَتَفَلَ صَلَّى اللهُ عَلَيْهِ وَسَلَّمَ فِى الْمَاءِ الْمَالِحِ ، فَصَارَ عَذْباً كَالْمِيَاهِ النِّيلِيَّةِ ،

١٩. وَأَشْبَعَ صَلَّى اللهُ عَلَيْهِ وَسَلَّمَ أَهْلَ الصُّفَّةِ وَهُمْ يَزِيدُونَ عَنِ السَّبْعِينَ مِنْ

satiated with it. Abū Hurayra ﷺ also drank to his fill, then exclaimed, 'By Allāh! I do not find the milk to have diminished, not even by a sip, O Rasul Allāh!'

20. Rocks became soft under his noble feet ﷺ, as if it were wet, soft soil. And when he ﷺ walked in the sand, his feet did not sink in it

How many injured individuals were cured through his touch, his saliva, and his ﷺ supplications of seeking refuge! And how many who were ill; through the blessing of his touch and saliva, were given well-being and healing by Allāh!

21. From his miracles ﷺ, is that his voice could be heard from a distance, and whoever desired to listen to his wise counsel was able to hear him. This fact is mentioned by al-Bayḥaqī ﷺ in his book, *Dalāʾil al-Nubuwwa*

22. An aroma emanated from him ﷺ, which was much sweeter than any perfume

23. His light ﷺ was more radiant than the sun and brighter than all other heavenly luminous objects. And this has not changed, even till now

How fortunate is the one who has smelled his scent, and perceived him with the eyes of the heart and saw him ﷺ (with their physical eyes). Especially while standing and facing the elevated, pure, honored *Rawda*, while visiting him ﷺ with his soul and his heart. O my brother, this is an indication for the one who understands this speech of mine and is attentive to it.

قَدَحِ لَبَنٍ وَشَبِعَ أَبُو هُرَيْرَةَ رَضِيَ اللهُ عَنْهُ حَتَّى قَالَ: وَاللهِ لَا أَجِدُ فِيهَا مَوْضِعَ مَذْقَةٍ يَا رَسُولَ اللهِ ،

٢٠. وَلَانَ الْحَجَرُ تَحْتَ قَدَمَيْهِ الشَّرِيفَتَيْنِ ، كَأَنَّهُ طِينَةٌ لَازِبَةٌ طَرِيَّةٌ ، وَإِذَا مَشَى صَلَّى اللهُ عَلَيْهِ وَسَلَّمَ عَلَى الرَّمْلِ فَلَا تَغُوصُ فِيهِ قَدَمَاهُ ،

وَكَمْ أَبْرَأَتْ وَصَباً بِاللَّمْسِ رَاحَتُهُ صَلَّى اللهُ عَلَيْهِ وَسَلَّمَ ، وَرِيقُهُ ، وَدَعَوَاتُهُ التَّعَوُّذِيَّةُ ، فَكَمْ مِنْ مَرِيضٍ بِبَرَكَةِ لَمْسِهِ وَرِيقِهِ صَلَّى اللهُ عَلَيْهِ وَسَلَّمَ عَافَاهُ اللهُ وَشَفَاهُ ،

٢١. وَمِنْ مُعْجِزَاتِهِ صَلَّى اللهُ عَلَيْهِ وَسَلَّمَ أَنَّ صَوْتَهُ يُسْمَعُ مِنْ بُعْدٍ ، وَيَسْمَعُهُ كُلُّ مَنْ قَصَدَهُ صَلَّى اللهُ عَلَيْهِ وَسَلَّمَ بِكَلِمَاتِهِ الْحِكَمِيَّةِ ، ذَكَرَ ذَلِكَ الْبَيْهَقِيُّ رَحِمَهُ اللهُ فِي دَلَائِلِ النُّبُوَّةِ

٢٢. وَحَكَاهُ ، وَكَانَ صَلَّى اللهُ عَلَيْهِ وَسَلَّمَ يَفُوحُ مِنْهُ طِيبٌ أَطْيَبُ مِنَ الطِّيبِ

٢٣. وَيَعْلُوهُ نُورٌ أَضْوَأُ مِنَ الشَّمْسِ وَالْأَنْوَارِ الْقَمَرِيَّةِ ، وَلَا يَزَالُ صَلَّى اللهُ عَلَيْهِ وَسَلَّمَ ، كَذَلِكَ حَتَّى الْآنَ ،

وَيَا سَعْدَ مَنْ شَمَّ طِيبَهُ صَلَّى اللهُ عَلَيْهِ وَسَلَّمَ وَأَبْصَرَهُ بِعَيْنَيْ قَلْبِهِ وَرَآهُ ، لَا سِيَّمَا

O Allāh send blessings, peace and abundance on our liege and master, Muḥammad, the best of creation, and on his family, in every glance and breath, as many times as all that is contained in the knowledge of Allāh.

عِنْدَ وُقُوفِهِ تُجَاهَ الرَّوْضَةِ الشَّرِيفَةِ النَّجْدِيَّةِ الزَّكِيَّةِ ، وَزَارَهُ صَلَّى اللهُ عَلَيْهِ وَسَلَّمَ بِرُوحِهِ وَقَلْبِهِ . هَذَا يَا أَخَانَا إِشَارَةٌ لِمَنْ عَرَفَ كَلَامِي هَذَا وَوَعَاهُ ،

﴿اللّٰهُمَّ صَلِّ وَسَلِّمْ وَبَارِكْ عَلَى سَيِّدِنَا وَمَوْلَانَا مُحَمَّدٍ خَيْرِ الْبَرِيَّةِ،
وَعَلَى آلِهِ فِي كُلِّ لَمْحَةٍ وَنَفَسٍ عَدَدَ مَا وَسِعَهُ عِلْمُ اللهِ﴾

CHAPTER 23

Concerning His Love ﷺ

Know [this]! No one can be a true believer until the Messenger of Allāh ﷺ becomes more beloved to him than his own soul, his children, his parents, and all humanity; as love of him is love for Allāh and obedience to him is obedience to Allāh. Do not be heedless regarding the selected and chosen one of Allāh ﷺ.

And from the signs of love for him ﷺ is to send an abundance of [prayers of] salutations and blessings upon him, every morning and evening. And [from the signs is] the visitation of the honorable *Rawda*, which no believer pays a visit to it except his chest is expanded and his heart is delighted whenever he says: *May peace be upon you O my master, O Messenger of Allāh.*

And love for him [also includes] love for his *Ahl al-Bayt* ﷺ, for they are the pure prophetic relatives. Also from this love, is love for his companions ﷺ who are the guiding leaders, along with visiting their graves, because it is a verbal and practical sunna (meaning he instructed it and practiced it himself ﷺ).

The Prophet ﷺ visited the occupants of al-Baqīʿ, the martyrs of Badr, and also his paternal uncle, the leader of the martyrs, Sayyiduna Ḥamza ﷺ as it is narrated in the ḥadith. And he ﷺ used to visit the martyrs of Badr once every year, travelling from Madīna to Badr, as it is mentioned by Ibn Sayyid in his *Sīra* book.

الفصل الثالث والعشرون

فِى مَحَبَّتِهِ صَلَّى اللهُ عَلَيْهِ وَسَلَّمَ

وَاعْلَمْ أَنَّهُ لَا يُؤْمِنُ أَحَدٌ حَتَّى يَكُونَ رَسُولُ اللهِ صَلَّى اللهُ عَلَيْهِ وَسَلَّمَ أَحَبَّ إِلَيْهِ مِنْ نَفْسِهِ وَوَلَدِهِ وَوَالِدِهِ وَسَائِرِ الْخَلِيقَةِ الْإِنْسَانِيَّةِ ، إِذْ مَحَبَّتُهُ هِىَ مَحَبَّةُ اللهِ تَعَالَى ، وَطَاعَتُهُ هِىَ طَاعَةُ اللهِ تَعَالَى ، وَلَا تَغْفُلْ عَنْ صَفِيِّ اللهِ تَعَالَى وَمُجْتَبَاهُ، وَمِنْ أَدِلَّةِ مَحَبَّتِهِ صَلَّى اللهُ عَلَيْهِ وَسَلَّمَ كَثْرَةُ الصَّلَاةِ وَالسَّلَامِ عَلَيْهِ فِى الْبُكْرَةِ وَالْعَشِيَّةِ ، وَزِيَارَةُ رَوْضَتِهِ الشَّرِيفَةِ الَّتِى مَا زَارَهَا مُؤْمِنٌ إِلَّا انْشَرَحَ صَدْرُهُ ، وَفَرِحَ قَلْبُهُ عِنْدَمَا يَقُولُ: «السَّلَامُ عَلَيْكَ يَا سَيِّدِى يَا رَسُولَ اللهِ » .

وَمِنْ مَحَبَّتِهِ صَلَّى اللهُ عَلَيْهِ وَسَلَّمَ مَحَبَّةُ أَهْلِ بَيْتِهِ رَضِىَ اللهُ عَنْهُمْ ، وَهُمُ الْعِتْرَةُ الطَّاهِرَةُ النَّبَوِيَّةُ ، وَمَحَبَّةُ أَصْحَابِهِ الْأَئِمَّةِ الْهُدَاةِ ، وَزِيَارَةُ مَقَابِرِهِمْ ، لِأَنَّ زِيَارَةَ الْمَقَابِرِ سُنَّةٌ قَوْلِيَّةٌ وَفِعْلِيَّةٌ ، وَقَدْ زَارَ النَّبِيُّ صَلَّى اللهُ عَلَيْهِ وَسَلَّمَ أَهْلَ الْبَقِيعِ، وَشُهَدَاءَ بَدْرٍ ، وَعَمَّهُ حَمْزَةَ سَيِّدَ الشُّهَدَاءِ رَضِىَ اللهُ عَنْهُ ، كَمَا رَوَيْنَاهُ ، وَكَانَ صَلَّى اللهُ عَلَيْهِ وَسَلَّمَ يَزُورُ شُهَدَاءَ بَدْرٍ فِى كُلِّ عَامٍ مَرَّةً مُسَافِراً مِنَ الْمَدِينَةِ إِلَى بَدْرٍ ، ذَكَرَ ذَلِكَ ابْنُ سَيِّدِ النَّاسِ فِى سِيرَتِهِ النَّبَوِيَّةِ ، وَشَدُّ الرِّحَالِ إِلَى زِيَارَةِ النَّبِيِّ

And undertaking a journey to visit the Prophet ﷺ and visiting the righteous, while they are alive or after death, is from the sunna, because that which leads to the sunna is a sunna, as it is explained by Imām al-Nawawi.

As for the ḥadith which says, 'Do not undertake a journey except to the three *masājid*', this ḥadith is to elucidate the virtues of these masājid, not to prohibit visitations to other than them, as attested by the *'ulamā* of al-Azhar. The phrase 'do not undertake a journey' is excluded from being the dominant point, since the prohibition, as we have understood it, is from wandering from one masjid to another (thinking that there is more preference in performing prayer there as opposed to the first).

O my brother in Allāh! It is incumbent on you to visit the Prophet ﷺ and visit his *Ahl al-Bayt*, the Ṣaḥāba, and the righteous, for they are the people who possess lofty ranks. In fact, whoever visits and greets them, they see him (the visitor) and return the greetings. Glad tidings for the one who greets them with a sound heart, how fortunate is he! Especially the Imām, Abū 'Abd Allāh, our Master, al-Ḥusayn ﷺ and those who are with him in the surroundings of Egypt. Therefore, visit them with your soul and heart, and know that the [true] visit is with the souls not just by the bodies, O slave of Allāh!

O Allāh send blessings, peace and abundance on our liege and master, Muḥammad, the best of creation, and on his family, in every glance and breath, as many times as all that is contained in the knowledge of Allāh.

صَلَّى اللهُ عَلَيْهِ وَسَلَّمَ ، وَزِيَارَةِ الصَّالِحِينَ أَحْيَاءً وَأَمْوَاتاً سُنَّةٌ ، لِأَنَّ مَا وَصَّلَ إِلَى السُّنَّةِ فَهُوَ سُنَّةٌ ، كَمَا بَيَّنَهُ النَّوَوِيُّ وَحَكَاهُ ،

وَأَمَّا حَدِيثُ « لَا تُشَدُّ الرِّحَالُ » فَوَارِدٌ فِي بَيَانِ فَضْلِ الْمَسَاجِدِ وَلَيْسَ لِلنَّهْيِ عَنِ الزِّيَارَةِ ، كَمَا قَرَّرَهُ أَهْلُ الْعُلُومِ الْأَزْهَرِيَّةِ ، وَلَفْظُ « لَا تُشَدُّ الرِّحَالُ » خُرِّجَ مَخْرَجَ الغَالِبِ ، إِذْ الْمَنْهِيُّ عَنْهُ مُطْلَقُ الْاِنْتِقَالِ مِنْ مَسْجِدٍ إِلَى مَسْجِدٍ كَمَا فَهِمْنَاهُ ، وَعَلَيْكَ يَا أَخَانَا فِي اللهِ تَعَالَى بِزِيَارَةِ النَّبِيِّ صَلَّى اللهُ عَلَيْهِ وَسَلَّمَ ، وَزِيَارَةِ أَهْلِ بَيْتِهِ رَضِيَ اللهُ عَنْهُمْ ، وَالصَّحَابَةِ ، وَالصَّالِحِينَ ، أُولِي الدَّرَجَاتِ الْعَلِيَّةِ ، فَإِنَّ كُلَّ مَنْ زَارَهُمْ وَسَلَّمَ عَلَيْهِمْ رَأَوْهُ وَرَدُّوا سَلَامَهُ ، فَيَا سَعْدَ مَنْ سَلَّمَ عَلَيْهِمْ بِقَلْبٍ سَلِيمٍ ، وَيَا بُشْرَاهُ ، لَاسِيَّمَا الْإِمَامِ أَبِي عَبْدِ اللهِ الْحُسَيْنِ ، وَمَنْ مَعَهُ بِالدِّيَارِ الْمِصْرِيَّةِ ، فَزُرْهُمْ بِرُوحِكَ وَقَلْبِكَ ، وَاعْلَمْ أَنَّ الزِّيَارَةَ بِالْأَرْوَاحِ لَا بِالْأَشْبَاحِ يَا عَبْدَ اللهِ ،

﴿اللَّهُمَّ صَلِّ وَسَلِّمْ وَبَارِكْ عَلَى سَيِّدِنَا وَمَوْلَانَا مُحَمَّدٍ خَيْرِ الْبَرِيَّةِ،
وَعَلَى آلِهِ فِي كُلِّ لَمْحَةٍ وَنَفَسٍ عَدَدَ مَا وَسِعَهُ عِلْمُ اللهِ﴾

CHAPTER 24

Visiting Him ﷺ at His Noble Rawda in Madīna

As for visiting the Prophet ﷺ at his honored Rawda, this is *wajib* (obligatory) according to some scholars of the Islāmic Umma, and others say that it is sunna. The latter verdict is of the four imāms.

It has come in narrations that he ﷺ replies to the greeting of the one who greets him at the noble Rawda and what a great privilege this is!

And he ﷺ will intercede for whoever visits him, an intercession that will cause the beneficiary to enter Paradise and obtain everlasting bliss. The beneficiary will then be delighted and happy.

My soul has achieved its desire,
These are the lights of ṬāḤā, the Arab.

These lights of his have become apparent,
And has become visible from behind those veils.

Rejoice, O Soul, this is *al-Mustafa* (the chosen one),
The seal of the Messengers, the very best of the Arabs.

O Messenger of Allāh, surely I am a sinner,

الفصل الرابع والعشرون

فِي زِيَارَتِهِ صَلَّى اللهُ عَلَيْهِ وَسَلَّمَ فِي رَوْضَتِهِ الشَّرِيفَةِ

وَأَمَّا زِيَارَتُهُ صَلَّى اللهُ عَلَيْهِ وَسَلَّمَ فِي رَوْضَتِهِ الشَّرِيفَةِ فَقَدْ أَوْجَبَ ذَلِكَ بَعْضُ عُلَمَاءِ الْأُمَّةِ الْإِسْلَامِيَّةِ، وَقِيلَ: سُنَّةٌ، وَهَذَا الْقَوْلُ كُلٌّ مِنَ الْأَئِمَّةِ الْأَرْبَعَةِ قَالَ بِهِ وَارْتَضَاهُ، وَقَدْ وَرَدَ أَنَّهُ صَلَّى اللهُ عَلَيْهِ وَسَلَّمَ يَرُدُّ السَّلَامَ عَلَى مَنْ سَلَّمَ عَلَيْهِ عِنْدَ الرَّوْضَةِ الشَّرِيفَةِ، فَيَالَهَا مِنْ مَزِيَّةٍ، وَيَشْفَعُ صَلَّى اللهُ عَلَيْهِ وَسَلَّمَ لِكُلِّ مَنْ زَارَهُ شَفَاعَةً تُدْخِلُ صَاحِبَهَا الْجَنَّةَ، وَيَنَالُ مِنَ الْخُلْدِ أَعْلَاهُ، وَيَكُونُ عِنْدَ ذَلِكَ فَرِحاً مَسْرُوراً:

مُهْجَتِي قَدْ نِلْتَ كُلَّ الْأَرَبِ ... هَذِهِ أَنْوَارُ طَهَ الْعَرَبِي
هَذِهِ أَنْوَارُهُ قَدْ ظَهَرَتْ ... وَبَدَتْ مِنْ خَلْفِ تِلْكَ الْحُجُبِ
أَبْشِرِي يَا نَفْسُ هَذَا الْمُصْطَفَى ... خَاتَمُ الرُّسْلِ خِيَارُ الْعَرَبِ
يَا رَسُولَ اللهِ إِنِّي مُذْنِبٌ ... وَمِنَ الْجُودِ قَبُولُ الْمُذْنِبِ

وَأَنَّ مَنْ زَارَهُ صَلَّى اللهُ عَلَيْهِ وَسَلَّمَ يُكْسَى حُلَلاً مِنَ النُّورِ مُطَرَّزَةً بِالْأَنْوَارِ

> And from the requirements of generosity is to accept the sinner.

And whoever visits him ﷺ will be clothed with a garment embellished with majestic radiance. He will drink the drink of the gnostics, and his soul will derive light until he recognizes the one, who is in front of him, who honors him, and gives him to drink (spiritually).

The scholars have said: Whatever leads you to a sunna, is also a sunna. Therefore walking or undertaking a journey to visit him ﷺ will be a practical sunna, meaning the one who does so would be given the reward of acting on a sunna. This is because the Prophet ﷺ visited the graves (as mentioned earlier) and commanded [others] to visit them. As such, this is a verbal and practical sunna. How fortunate is that person who revives the sunna of the Messenger of Allāh ﷺ!

He ﷺ has said "The space between my pulpit and the apartment of ʿĀʾisha ؓ is a garden from the gardens of Paradise." The commentators of [*Sahih*] al-Bukhari have stated that it is in reality a garden of Paradise (not a metaphor). O my brother in Allāh! Wouldn't you like to perform prayer in Paradise! So that you will be among those whom his Lord loves and who loves his Lord!

And his masjid is honored because of its connection to him ﷺ. As such, prayers in it, whether voluntary or obligatory, are multiplied by one thousand.

'Whoever performs forty prayers [consecutively] in his masjid, Allāh will decree for him freedom from punishment, hypocrisy and Hellfire.' This ḥadith is narrated by Imām Aḥmad ؒ in his compilation.

Had it not been for him ﷺ, his masjid would be like any other masjid without any extra virtue or merit. The Messenger of Allāh ﷺ

الْجَلَالِيَّةِ ، وَيَشْرَبُ شَرَابَ الْعَارِفِينَ ، فَتَسْتَنِيرُ رُوحُهُ حَتَّى يَعْرِفَ مَنْ وَقَفَ بَيْنَ يَدَيْهِ ، وَمَنْ أَكْرَمَهُ وَسَقَاهُ ، وَقَدْ قَالَ الْعُلَمَاءُ : مَا وَصَلَ إِلَى السُّنَّةِ فَهُوَ سُنَّةٌ، فَالْمَشْيُ أَوْ شَدُّ الرَّحْلِ إِلَى زِيَارَتِهِ صَلَّى اللهُ عَلَيْهِ وَسَلَّمَ سُنَّةٌ فِعْلِيَّةٌ ، أَىْ يُثَابُ فَاعِلُهَا ثَوَابَ السُّنَّةِ ، لِأَنَّهُ صَلَّى اللهُ عَلَيْهِ وَسَلَّمَ زَارَ الْمَقَابِرَ ، وَأَمَرَ بِزِيَارَتِهَا ، فَهِىَ سُنَّةٌ قَوْلِيَّةٌ وَفِعْلِيَّةٌ ، فَيَا سَعْدَ مَنْ أَحْيَا سُنَّةَ رَسُولِ اللهِ ،

وَقَالَ صَلَّى اللهُ عَلَيْهِ وَسَلَّمَ :« مَا بَيْنَ مِنْبَرِى وَبَيْتِ عَائِشَةَ رَوْضَةٌ مِنْ رِيَاضِ الْجَنَّةِ » وَقَدْ قَالَ شُرَّاحُ الْبُخَارِيِّ : هِىَ رَوْضَةٌ حَقِيقِيَّةٌ ، فَهَلْ لَكَ يَا أَخَانَا فِى اللهِ تَعَالَى أَنْ تُصَلِّىَ فِى الْجَنَّةِ ، فَتَكُونَ مِمَّنْ أَحَبَّهُ رَبُّهُ وَحَبَاهُ ،

وَقَدْ تَشَرَّفَ مَسْجِدُهُ صَلَّى اللهُ عَلَيْهِ وَسَلَّمَ بِنِسْبَتِهِ إِلَيْهِ ، فَصَارَتِ الصَّلَاةُ فِيهِ بِأَلْفٍ سَوَاءٌ كَانَتْ فَرْضِيَّةً أَوْ نَفْلِيَّةً ، « وَمَنْ صَلَّى فِى مَسْجِدِهِ صَلَّى اللهُ عَلَيْهِ وَسَلَّمَ أَرْبَعِينَ صَلَاةً كَتَبَ اللهُ لَهُ بَرَاءَةً مِنَ الْعَذَابِ وَمِنَ النِّفَاقِ وَمِنَ النَّارِ» أَخْرَجَهُ الْإِمَامُ أَحْمَدُ وَرَوَاهُ ، وَلَوْلَاهُ صَلَّى اللهُ عَلَيْهِ وَسَلَّمَ لَكَانَ مَسْجِدُهُ كَبَقِيَّةِ الْمَسَاجِدِ بِلَا فَضْلٍ وَلَا مَزِيَّةٍ ، وَرَسُولُ اللهُ صَلَّى اللهُ عَلَيْهِ وَسَلَّمَ أَفْضَلُ مِنَ الْعَرْشِ وَالْكُرْسِيِّ وَالْكَعْبَةِ وَجَمِيعِ الْمَسَاجِدِ ، وَمِنْ نَعِيمِ الْجَنَّةِ وَمَا حَوَاهُ ،

وَيَسْمَعُ السَّلَامَ وَيَرُدُّهُ ، فَلَا تَكُنْ شَاكًّا فِى ذَلِكَ ، فَتَقَعَ فِى عَقِيدَةِ الْجَاهِلِيَّةِ ، لِأَنَّهُمْ يَقُولُونَ الْمَيِّتُ إِذَا مَاتَ لَا يَسْمَعُ وَلَا يُبْصِرُ ، وَلَا يَصِلُ إِلَيْهِ ثَوَابٌ ، وَلَا

is more superior than the Throne, the Footstool, the Ka'ba and all the masājid, and all the heavenly bounties of Paradise and whatever it contains!

And he hears the greetings and replies to them, so have no doubt about that and fall into the beliefs of ignorance! They (the polytheists) used to say, "When the person is dead, he does not hear or see, and no reward will reach him, nor will he be resurrected, and he becomes dust and that is his end and his termination."

As you enter his masjid ﷺ, your heart will feel an increase of faith and tranquillity, especially while facing him ﷺ and conveying greetings. And how many are the lovers for whom the light elevated them, and their eyes flowed with tears out of intense joy!

As often as the soul recollects the memory of the Rawda, it is almost as if it flies out of the physical realm and yearns to be in Madīna, facing the blessed grave in the masjid of the Messenger of Allāh ﷺ.

Al-Ḥāfiẓ al-Suyūṭī ؓ has narrated with his *sanad*, that when Sayyid Aḥmad al-Rifā'ī ؓ visited the Prophet ﷺ, he presented two couplets that indicated the lofty status of his pure soul ﷺ. On hearing the couplets, the Prophet ﷺ extended his blessed hand and Sayyid Aḥmad ؓ kissed it while people were looking on. No one kissed it other than him.

The couplets are as follows:

> While I was distant from you, I used to send my soul as my deputy,
> To kiss the earth in front of you on my behalf.
>
> Now this soul is physically present here before you,
> therefore stretch forth your hand so that my lips can derive pleasure (by kissing them).

يُبْعَثُ ، وَيَصِيرُ تُرَاباً وَهَذِهِ نِهَايَتُهُ وَمُنْتَهَاهُ ،

وَإِذَا دَخَلْتَ مَسْجِدَهُ صَلَّى اللهُ عَلَيْهِ وَسَلَّمَ أَحَسَّ قَلْبُكَ بِزِيَادَةِ الْإِيمَانِ وَالطُّمَأْنِينَةِ ، لَا سِيَّمَا عِنْدَ مُوَاجَهَتِهِ وَإِلْقَاءِ التَّحِيَّةِ ، وَكَمْ مِنْ مُحِبٍّ قَدْ عَلَاهُ النُّورُ ، وَفَاضَتْ مِنْ شِدَّةِ الْفَرَحِ بِالدُّمُوعِ عَيْنَاهُ ،

فَيَالَهَا مِنْ سَاعَةٍ كُلَّمَا ذَكَرَتْهَا الرُّوحُ تَكَادُ أَنْ تَطِيرَ مِنْ عَالَمِ الْجِسْمَانِيَّةِ، وَتَتَمَنَّى أَنْ تَكُونَ بِالْمَدِينَةِ تُجَاهَ الرَّوْضَةِ الشَّرِيفَةِ فِي مَسْجِدِ رَسُولِ اللهِ ، وَقَدْ أَخْرَجَ الْحَافِظُ السُّيُوطِيُّ رَحِمَهُ اللهُ بِسَنَدِهِ أَنَّ السَّيِّدَ أَحْمَدَ الرِّفَاعِيَّ رَضِيَ اللهُ عَنْهُ لَمَّا زَارَ النَّبِيَّ صَلَّى اللهُ عَلَيْهِ وَسَلَّمَ وَأَسْمَعَهُ بَيْتَيْنِ مِنَ الشِّعْرِ يَدُلَّانِ عَلَى عُلُوِّ رُوحِهِ التَّقِيَّةِ ، أَخْرَجَ لَهُ صَلَّى اللهُ عَلَيْهِ وَسَلَّمَ يَدَهُ الشَّرِيفَةَ ، فَقَبَّلَهَا وَالنَّاسُ يَنْظُرُونَ ، وَمَا قَبَّلَهَا أَحَدٌ سِوَاهُ ، وَالْبَيْتَانِ هُمَا :

فِي حَالَـةِ الْبُعْـدِ رُوحِي كُنْتُ أُرْسِـلُهَا   تُقَبِّـلُ الْأَرْضَ عَـنِّي وَهْيَ نَائِبَـتِي
وَهَـذِهِ دَوْلَـةُ الْأَشْـبَاحِ قَـدْ حَـضَرَتْ   فَامْـدُدْ يَمِينَـكَ كَيْ تَحْظَـى بِهَا شَـفَتِي

وَقَالَ سَيِّدِي ابْنُ السَّنُوسِيِّ رَضِيَ اللهُ عَنْهُ: لَمْ يَكُنْ لِشَيْخِي السَّيِّدِ أَحْمَدَ ابْنِ إِدْرِيسَ رَضِيَ اللهُ عَنْهُ مُعَوَّلٌ عَلَى أَحَدٍ مِنَ الْخَلْقِ فِي أَوَّلِ أَمْرِهِ ، وَأَوْسَطِهِ ، وَآخِرِهِ إِلَّا عَلَى خَيْرِ الْبَرِيَّةِ ، وَقَدْ أَخْبَرَ السَّيِّدُ ابْنُ إِدْرِيسَ رَضِيَ اللهُ عَنْهُ بِأَنَّهُ تَلَقَّى

My master, [Shaykh] Ibn al-Sanūsī ؓ, said, "My shaykh, Sayyid Aḥmad b. Idrīs, never relied on anyone in all creation, whether in the beginning, middle or the end of his affair except the best of creation ﷺ. Sayyid Aḥmad b. Idrīs ؓ informed us that he received all his litanies in a wakeful state from our master, the Messenger of Allāh ﷺ. And he asked the Prophet ﷺ to take charge of the upbringing of those who join the Aḥmadiyya [spiritual] path. And he ﷺ agreed to that. He (Aḥmad b. Idrīs) would say, 'We have turned you over to one who is better than us.'" So how fortunate and glad tidings to those who take his path and read his litanies!

When Sayyid Muḥammad 'Uthmān al-Mīrghanī ؓ used to greet the Prophet ﷺ in prayer, while he was in the lands of Ethiopia, he would hear the reply from the Prophet ﷺ and his ears were honored to hear him ﷺ.

Sayyid Ibn al-Sanūsī ؓ once asked the Prophet ﷺ, "Where is Sayyiduna Abū Bakr al-Ṣiddīq?" The Prophet ﷺ said to him, "He is with your shaykh, al-Shifā'," meaning, Aḥmad b. Idrīs ؓ, the man of inspired knowledge.

Imām al-Suyūṭī ؓ used to discuss ḥadith with the Prophet ﷺ while awake. Likewise, he mentioned and narrated that this occurred for many of the prominent scholars.

My master, Aḥmad [b. Idrīs] ؓ, gave glad tidings to those who took his path, that they will be able to see him ﷺ while awake and in a dream; he mentioned that in regards to al-Ṣalāt al-'Aẓīmiyya. And many of the murids have obtained that privilege, especially those who recite al-Ṣalāt al-'Aẓīmiyya in abundance, as well as the fourteen *Ṣalawāt* [of Shaykh Aḥmad b. Idrīs]. Therefore, you should increase [your recitation] until you [also] behold the best of creation and meet with him ﷺ.

جَمِيعَ أَوْرَادِهِ يَقظَةً عَنْ سَيِّدِنَا رَسُولِ اللهِ ، وَسَأَلَ النَّبِيَّ صَلَّى اللهُ عَلَيْهِ وَسَلَّمَ أَنْ يَتَوَلَّى تَرْبِيَةَ الآخِذِينَ لِطَرِيقَتِهِ الْأَحْمَدِيَّةِ ، فَقبِلَ مِنْهُ صَلَّى اللهُ عَلَيْهِ وَسَلَّمَ ذَلِكَ ، وَكَانَ رَضِيَ اللهُ عَنْهُ يَقُولُ : حَوَّلْنَاكُمْ إِلَى مَنْ هُوَ خَيْرٌ مِنَّا ، فَيَا سَعْدَ مَنْ أَخَذَ طَرِيقَهُ وَتَلَا وِرْدَهُ وَيَا بُشْرَاهُ ،

وَكَانَ السَّيِّدُ مُحَمَّدُ عُثْمَانَ الْمِيرْغَنِيُّ يُسَلِّمُ عَلَى النَّبِيِّ صَلَّى اللهُ عَلَيْهِ وَسَلَّمَ فِي الصَّلَاةِ وَهُوَ فِي البِلَادِ الْحَبَشِيَّةِ ، فَيَسْمَعُ الرَّدَّ مِنْهُ صَلَّى اللهُ عَلَيْهِ وَسَلَّمَ وَتَتَشَرَّفُ بِهِ أُذُنَاهُ ،

وَقَالَ سَيِّدِي ابْنُ السَّنُوسِيِّ رَضِيَ اللهُ عَنْهُ مَرَّةً لِلنَّبِيِّ صَلَّى اللهُ عَلَيْهِ وَسَلَّمَ : أَيْنَ سَيِّدُنَا أَبُو بَكْرٍ الصِّدِّيقُ رَضِيَ اللهُ عَنْهُ ؟ فَقَالَ لَهُ النَّبِيُّ صَلَّى اللهُ عَلَيْهِ وَسَلَّمَ : هُوَ مَعَ شَيْخِكَ الشِّفَاءِ ، أَيْ ابْنِ إِدْرِيسَ ذِي الْعُلُومِ اللَّدُنِّيَّةِ ،

وَكَانَ السُّيُوطِيُّ رَحِمَهُ اللهُ يَتَذَاكَرُ مَعَ النَّبِيِّ صَلَّى اللهُ عَلَيْهِ وَسَلَّمَ الْحَدِيثَ يَقَظَةً كَمَا ذَكَرَ ذَلِكَ كَثِيرٌ مِنَ الْعُلَمَاءِ الْأَجِلَّاءِ وَحَكَاهُ، وَقَدْ بَشَّرَ سَيِّدِي أَحْمَدُ رَضِيَ اللهُ عَنْهُ الآخِذِينَ طَرِيقَهُ بِرُؤْيَتِهِ صَلَّى اللهُ عَلَيْهِ وَسَلَّمَ فِي الْيَقَظَةِ وَفِي المَنَامِ، وَقَدْ ذَكَرَ ذَلِكَ فِي الصَّلَاةِ الْعَظِيمِيَّةِ ، وَقَدْ حَصَلَ ذَلِكَ لِكَثِيرٍ مِنْهُمْ لَا سِيَّمَا لِلْمُكْثِرِينَ للصَّلَاةِ الْعَظِيمِيَّةِ ، وَالصَّلَوَاتِ الأَرْبَعَ عَشْرَةِ ، فَأَكْثِرْ كَمَا أَكْثَرُوا حَتَّى تُشَاهِدَ خَيْرَ الْبَرِيَّةِ صَلَّى اللهُ عَلَيْهِ وَسَلَّمَ وَتَلْقَاهُ ،

O Allāh send blessings, peace and abundance on our liege and master, Muḥammad, the best of creation, and on his family, in every glance and breath, as many times as all that is contained in the knowledge of Allāh.

﴿اللّٰهُمَّ صَلِّ وَسَلِّمْ وَبَارِكْ عَلَى سَيِّدِنَا وَمَوْلَانَا مُحَمَّدٍ خَيْرِ الْبَرِيَّةِ،
وَعَلَى آلِهِ فِي كُلِّ لَمْحَةٍ وَنَفَسٍ عَدَدَ مَا وَسِعَهُ عِلْمُ اللهِ﴾

CHAPTER 25

The Following of the Four Imāms

The scholars of the noble Azhar transmit that it is incumbent to follow one of the four *imāms* of the schools of fiqh. Especially for those that did not study the Qurʾān and the sunna, and do not have the understanding of the Qurʾān's directives and its guidance.

Likewise, it is incumbent upon everyone to follow Imām al-Ashʿarī ﷺ, as far as *tawḥīd* and *ʿaqīda* is concerned. Whoever says, 'I am a *mujtahid*' and he has not reached the level of *ijtihad* (analogical deduction) then certainly he is fabricating a lie against Allāh.

Knowledge is acquired from the hearts of men and not from books. Therefore, it is necessary to seek it and endure patiently with the long time it takes to know the secrets of the Qurʾān and what it encompasses.

Beware of labelling Muslims as disbelievers and attributing the verses that came regarding the polytheists, to the Muslims, thus charging them with disbelief and idolatry. Indeed, this is from the traits of the *Khawārij*, as Imām al-Bukhari ﷺ has mentioned in his book [*Sahih al-Bukhari*] under the chapter 'Traits of the Khawārij.'

Beware of making Allāh similar with His creation, because it is the trait of the anthropomorphists, who are the people of gross misguidance.

الفصل الخامس والعشرون

اتِّبَاعُ الْأَئِمَّةِ الْأَرْبَعَةِ رَضِىَ اللهُ عَنْهُمْ

وَقَدْ نَصَّ عُلَمَاءُ الْأَزْهَرِ الشَّرِيفِ عَلَى وُجُوبِ اتِّبَاعِ إِمَامٍ مِنَ الْأَئِمَّةِ الْأَرْبَعَةِ أَهْلِ الْمَذَاهِبِ الْفِقْهِيَّةِ ، وَلَا سِيَّمَا الَّذِينَ لَمْ يَدْرُسُوا الْكِتَابَ وَالسُّنَّةَ ، وَلَمْ يَعْرِفُوا مِنَ الْقُرْآنِ هَدْيَهُ وَهُدَاهُ ،

وَكَذَلِكَ يَجِبُ عَلَى كُلِّ وَاحِدٍ مُتَابَعَةُ الْأَشْعَرِيِّ فِى الْعَقَائِدِ التَّوْحِيدِيَّةِ ، وَمَنْ قَالَ إِنِّى مُجْتَهِدٌ وَلَمْ يَبْلُغْ دَرَجَةَ الاجْتِهَادِ فَإِنَّهُ مِمَّنْ افْتَرَى عَلَى اللهِ ، وَالْعِلْمُ يُؤْخَذُ مِنْ صُدُورِ الرِّجَالِ لَا مِنَ الْكُتُبِ الْمَطْوِيَّةِ، فَلِذَلِكَ يَجِبُ طَلَبُهُ وَالصَّبْرُ عَلَيْهِ مَعَ طُولِ زَمَانٍ لِيَعْرِفَ أَسْرَارَ الْقُرْآنِ وَمَا حَوَاهُ، وَإِيَّاكَ وَتَكْفِيرَ الْمُسْلِمِينَ وَوَصْفَهُمْ بِالْآيَاتِ الْوَارِدَةِ فِى الْمُشْرِكِينَ وَرَمْيَهُمْ بِالْكُفْرِ وَالْوَثَنِيَّةِ ، فَإِنَّ ذَلِكَ مِنْ صِفَةِ الْخَوَارِجِ ، كَمَا رَوَى ذَلِكَ الْبُخَارِيُّ فِى بَابِ صِفَةِ الْخَوَارِجِ وَحَكَاهُ ،

وَإِيَّاكَ وَتَشْبِيهَ اللهِ تَعَالَى بِخَلْقِهِ فَإِنَّ ذَلِكَ مِنْ صِفَاتِ الْمُجَسِّمَةِ أَهْلِ الضَّلَالَةِ الظُّلْمَانِيَّةِ ، وَإِياكَ وَإِنْكَارَ جَاهِ رَسُولِ اللهِ صَلَّى اللهُ عَلَيْهِ وَسَلَّمَ فَإِنَّ جَاهَهُ

Beware of rejecting the rank of the Prophet ﷺ, since his rank is beneficial in this world and the day the servant meets his Creator and Lord ﷻ. Beware of objecting to the visitation of the graves of the righteous, because to reject it is ignorance and calamity. As for those things that are in opposition to the Qur'ān and sunna, the Sharī'a dislikes and refuses them.

As for the visitation of women to the graves, then this is also [from the] sunna as expounded on by al-Bukhari ﷺ, and this exposition results in the judgement that it is sunna.

And when a woman's *'awra* (nakedness) is exposed then it is not permissible for her to go out of her house, even for *Ḥajj* or making *ṭawāf* around the House of Allāh. In this time, the exposing of one's nudity has increased and become a widespread tribulation. It is forbidden for the perpetrator of nudity, the one who endorses it, and the one pleased with it. And due to this, Allāh is angry, calamities descend, the blessings of the land are removed, and the angels of mercy do not enter where there is a woman whose arms are not covered or her hair is exposed as it is mentioned in the sunna and as we have explained.

O Allāh pardon the Muslim men and women and guide them to the straight path of the Sharī'a, and remove from them all that You dislike and disapprove of.

O Allāh send blessings, peace and abundance on our liege and master, Muḥammad, the best of creation, and on his family, in every glance and breath, as many times as all that is contained in the knowledge of Allāh.

صَلَّى اللهُ عَلَيْهِ وَسَلَّمَ نَافِعٌ فِي الدُّنْيَا وَيَوْمَ يَلْقَى الْعَبْدُ خَالِقَهُ وَمَوْلَاهُ ، وَإِيَّاكَ وَالْإِنْكَارَ عَلَى زِيَارَةِ قُبُورِ الصَّالِحِينَ فَإِنَّ الْإِنْكَارَ جَهَالَةٌ وَبَلِيَّةٌ ، وَأَمَّا مَا يُخَالِفُ الْكِتَابَ وَالسُّنَّةَ فَإِنَّ الشَّرْعَ يَكْرَهُهُ وَيَأْبَاهُ ،

وَأَمَّا زِيَارَةُ النِّسَاءِ لِلْمَقَابِرِ فَسُنَّةٌ كَمَا تَرْجَمَ الْبُخَارِيُّ لِذَلِكَ تَرْجَمَةً تُفِيدُ حُكْمَ السُّنِّيَّةِ ، وَأَمَّا إِذَا كَانَتِ الْمَرْأَةُ عَارِيَةً فَلَا يَجُوزُ خُرُوجُهَا مِنْ بَيْتِهَا وَلَوْ إِلَى الْحَجِّ وَالطَّوَافِ بِبَيْتِ اللهِ ، وَقَدْ كَثُرَ الْعُرْيُ فِي هَذَا الزَّمَانِ وَعَمَّتْ بِهِ الْبَلِيَّةُ ، وَالْحُرْمَةُ عَلَى فَاعِلَتِهِ وَعَلَى مَنْ أَقَرَّهُ وَارْتَضَاهُ ، وَبِسَبَبِهِ يَغْضَبُ اللهُ تَعَالَى وَتَنْزِلُ الْبَلَايَا وَتَذْهَبُ الْبَرَكَاتُ الْأَرْضِيَّةُ ، وَمَلَائِكَةُ الرَّحْمَةِ لَا تَدْخُلُ بَيْتاً فِيهِ امْرَأَةٌ حَاسِرَةُ الذِّرَاعَيْنِ أَوْ عَارِيَةُ الرَّأْسِ كَمَا ثَبَتَ فِي السُّنَّةِ وَبَيَّنَّاهُ ،

اللَّهُمَّ تُبْ عَلَى الْمُسْلِمِينَ وَالْمُسْلِمَاتِ وَاهْدِهِمْ إِلَى الطَّرِيقَةِ الْمُسْتَقِيمَةِ الشَّرْعِيَّةِ، وَارْفَعْ عَنْهُمْ كُلَّ مَا تَكْرَهُهُ وَتَأْبَاهُ ،

﴿اللَّهُمَّ صَلِّ وَسَلِّمْ وَبَارِكْ عَلَى سَيِّدِنَا وَمَوْلَانَا مُحَمَّدٍ خَيْرِ الْبَرِيَّةِ،
وَعَلَى آلِهِ فِي كُلِّ لَمْحَةٍ وَنَفَسٍ عَدَدَ مَا وَسِعَهُ عِلْمُ اللهِ﴾

CHAPTER 26

Closing Du'ā

Your Lord ﷻ says: *Call upon me and I will answer you.* Therefore, raise your hands, humbly, O those who are present here, listening, [and reading], turning to Allāh with our hearts and with a sincere intention using as a means, the Prophet of mercy, His beloved and chosen one ﷺ.

O our Master, O Muḥammad, O Messenger of Allāh, surely we turn through you to Allāh, the Exalted, in Whose hands lies the fulfilment of all our needs, comprehensive and in detail, that You answer our supplication, fulfil our hopes and bestow us with what we ask for. O Allāh, allow his intercession on our behalf, an intercession that is accepted and You are pleased with, because there is no intercession for anyone except by the permission and pleasure of Allāh, the Exalted. We ask You, O Allāh, grant us pardon and well-being in religion, this world, and the Hereafter, and in our souls, intellects and in the limbs of the body and grant us success to do every good, through which Paradise becomes the abode and residence for the doer [of righteous deeds].

We ask You, O Allāh, for beneficial knowledge, a fearful heart, a glistening, emanating light, a comfortable life, sincere repentance that will erase all our open and hidden sins and all other sins we have perpetrated. Grant us chastity, security, good character and

الفصل السادس والعشرون

فِي دُعَاءِ الْخِتَامِ

وَقَالَ رَبُّكُمُ: ﴿ادْعُونِى أَسْتَجِبْ لَكُمْ﴾، فَارْفَعُوا أَكُفَّ الضَّرَاعَةِ يَا مَعْشَرَ الْحَاضِرِينَ وَالسَّامِعِينَ مُتَوَجِّهِينَ إِلَى اللهِ تَعَالَى بِالْقُلُوبِ، وَحُسْنِ النِّيَّةِ، مُتَوَسِّلِينَ إِلَيْهِ تَعَالَى بِنَبِيِّ الرَّحْمَةِ صَلَّى اللهُ عَلَيْهِ وَسَلَّمَ حَبِيبِهِ وَمُصْطَفَاهُ،

يَا سَيِّدَنَا يَا مُحَمَّدُ يَا رَسُولَ اللهِ إِنَّا تَوَجَّهْنَا بِكَ إِلَى اللهِ تَعَالَى مَنْ بِيَدِهِ قَضَاءُ الْحَوَائِجِ الْكُلِّيَّةِ وَالْجُزْئِيَّةِ، فِي أَنْ يُجِيبَ دُعَاءَنَا، وَيُحَقِّقَ رَجَاءَنَا وَيُعْطِيَنَا مَا سَأَلْنَاهُ، اللَّهُمَّ شَفِّعْهُ فِينَا شَفَاعَةً مَقْبُولَةً مَرْضِيَّةً، فَإِنَّهُ لَا شَفَاعَةَ لِأَحَدٍ إِلَّا بِإِذْنِ اللهِ تَعَالَى وَرِضَاهُ،

وَنَسْأَلُكَ اللَّهُمَّ الْعَفْوَ وَالْعَافِيَةَ فِي الدِّينِ وَالدُّنْيَا وَالْآخِرَةِ، وَالْأَرْوَاحِ وَالْعُقُولِ وَالْجَوَارِحِ الْبَدَنِيَّةِ، وَالتَّوْفِيقَ إِلَى كُلِّ خَيْرٍ مَنْ فَعَلَهُ كَانَتِ الْجَنَّةُ مُتَقَلَّبَهُ وَمَثْوَاهُ، وَنَسْأَلُكَ اللَّهُمَّ عِلْمًا نَافِعاً، وَقَلْباً خَاشِعاً، وَنُوراً سَاطِعاً، وَعِيشَةً هَنِيَّةً، وَتَوْبَةً نَصُوحاً تَمْحُو جَمِيعَ الْخَطَايَا الظَّاهِرَةِ وَالْخَفِيَّةِ، وَكُلَّ مَا ارْتَكَبْنَاهُ، وَعِفَّةً وَأَمَانَةً

the desire to do good. Grant us protection, assistance, expansion, generosity, honor and salvation. Grant us gnosis, and love that leads us to Your holy presence so that we may glorify You and remember You in abundance, together with every sincere person of remembrance.

And we ask You, O Allāh, to grant us an all-embracing mercy and a conclusive reformation for our children, wives, brethren and the entire Islāmic nation. Grant us Your ever-embracing bounty, and the mercy and independence of the Qurʾān; illuminate our hearts with the Qurʾānic words and verses, make it a proof in our favor and not against us, and guide us with its guidance and its directives. Do not cause us to be in opposition to the sunna of our Prophet ﷺ whether in word or deed, make him ﷺ pleased with us and attentive toward us, and let us drink at his fountain (*al-Ḥawḍ*), the water of which is the best of all waters. And join us and him ﷺ together just as you combined the soul (*rūḥ*) and spirit (*nafs*) in the physical form; and make him a soul for our essences in every aspect. And let us recognize his noble countenance the day we meet him ﷺ. Make us independent, by Your grace, from other than You, and grant us blessings in what You provided us from wealth and children, and make every difficulty in our affairs easy by Your power and might, for there is no power or might except by Allāh.

And seal us at the time of death with the seal of eternal bliss, illuminate our graves, and turn them into a garden from the gardens of Your Paradise. Refresh our souls with everlasting leisure and pleasure. And gather us on the Day of Resurrection in the assembly of the righteous, those whom the Great Terror will not grieve, the people of eternal felicity. And provide for us shade under Your Throne, on that day when there will be no other shade besides it.

O Allāh, allow Your Prophet ﷺ to intercede on our behalf. The owner of the grand intercession and the sublime station. For he ﷺ

وَحُسْنَ خُلُقٍ وَرَغْبَةً خَيْرِيَّةً ، وَالْحِفْظَ وَالنَّصْرَ وَالْبَسْطَ وَالسَّخَاءَ وَالإِكْرَامَ وَالنَّجَاةَ ، وَالْمَعْرِفَةَ وَالْمَحَبَّةَ الَّتِي تُوَصِّلُنَا إِلَى الْحَضْرَةِ الْقُدْسِيَّةِ ، كَيْ نُسَبِّحَكَ كَثِيراً نَذْكُرَكَ كَثِيراً مَعَ كُلِّ ذَاكِرٍ أَوَّاهٍ ،

وَنَسْأَلُكَ اللَّهُمَّ رَحْمَةً عَامَةً وَإِصْلَاحاً شَامِلاً لِذُرِّيَاتِنَا وَأَزْوَاجِنَا وَإِخْوَانِنَا وَسَائِرِ الْأُمَّةِ الْإِسْلَامِيَّةِ ، وَعُمَّنَا بِفَضْلِكَ الْعَظِيمِ ، وَرَحْمَةِ الْقُرْآنِ وَغِنَاهُ ، وَنَوِّرْ قُلُوبَنَا بِأَنْوَارِ كَلِمَاتِهِ وَآيَاتِهِ الْقُرْآنِيَّةِ ، وَاجْعَلْهُ حُجَّةً لَنَا ، وَلَا تَجْعَلْهُ حُجَّةً عَلَيْنَا ، وَاهْدِنَا بِهَدْيِهِ وَهُدَاهُ ، وَلَا تُخَالِفْ بِنَا عَنْ سُنَّةِ نَبِيِّنَا صَلَّى اللهُ عَلَيْهِ وَسَلَّمَ الْقَوْلِيَّةِ وَالْفِعْلِيَّةِ ، وَاجْعَلْهُ رَاضِياً عَنَّا وَمُقْبِلًا عَلَيْنَا وَأَوْرِدْنَا حَوْضَهُ الَّذِى هُوَ مِنْ أَفْضَلِ الْمِيَاهِ ، وَاجْمَعْ بَيْنَنَا وَبَيْنَهُ كَمَا جَمَعْتَ بَيْنَ الرُّوحِ وَالنَّفْسِ فِي الصُّورَةِ الْجِسْمَانِيَّةِ ، وَاجْعَلْهُ رُوحًا لِذَوَاتِنَا مِنْ جَمِيعِ الْوُجُوهِ ، وَعَرِّفْنَا وَجْهَهُ الْكَرِيمَ يَوْمَ نَلْقَاهُ ، وَأَغْنِنَا بِفَضْلِكَ عَمَّنْ سِوَاكَ ، وَبَارِكْ لَنَا فِيمَا رَزَقْتَنَا مِنَ الْمَالِ وَالذُّرِّيَّةِ ، وَيَسِّرْ عَسِيرَ أُمُورِنَا بِحَوْلِكَ وَقُوَّتِكَ ، فَإِنَّهُ لَا حَوْلَ وَلَا قُوَّةَ إِلَّا بِاللهِ ، وَاخْتِمْ لَنَا عِنْدَ الْمَمَاتِ بِخَاتِمَةِ السَّعَادَةِ السَّرْمَدِيَّةِ ، وَنَوِّرْ قُبُورَنَا ، وَاجْعَلْهَا رَوْضَةً مِنْ رِيَاضِ جَنَّتِكَ ، وَرَوِّحْ أَرْوَاحَنَا بِرَيْحَانِ الْخُلْدِ وَرُبَاهُ ، وَاحْشُرْنَا يَوْمَ الْقِيَامَةِ فِي زُمْرَةِ الصَّالِحِينَ الَّذِينَ لَا يَحْزُنُهُمُ الْفَزَعُ الْأَكْبَرُ أَهْلِ السَّعَادَةِ الْأَبَدِيَّةِ ، وَأَظِلَّنَا تَحْتَ ظِلِّ عَرْشِكَ الَّذِى لَا ظِلَّ يَوْمَئِذٍ سِوَاهُ ،

is the intercessor whose intercession is readily accepted and whose reputation and status are exalted.

And veil us, O Allāh, with Your graceful covering (of faults). O One Who manifests all that is beautiful and covers detestable actions, with His eternal mercy. Do not disgrace us, O Allāh, with regard to ourselves, our families, or our companions. O One Who there is no Lord other than Him, and there is no one worthy of worship other than Him. We seek refuge in You, O Allāh, from anxiety, grief, helplessness, laziness, cowardice, miserliness, overpowering of debts, being subjugated by men, and from base and lowly desires. And we seek refuge in You, O Allāh, from losing (Your) bounties, hastening of misfortune, constraining of the chest, and from evil conditions and circumstances.

We ask You, O Allāh, for all the good which our master Muḥammad ﷺ, the best of creation, has asked for, and we seek Your protection against all those evil matters that our master Muḥammad ﷺ, the Messenger of Allāh, had sought Your protection from.

O Allāh spread the Jaʿfariyya Aḥmadiyya Muḥammadiyya path all over the world with the methodology of [Shaykh] Ṣāliḥ al-Jaʿfarī, Allāh be pleased with him, the methodology You love and are pleased with.

Our path is the Qurʾān, the sunna, lessons of [religious] knowledge, recital of the Qurʾān, litanies, and the abundant remembrance of Allāh. On the path of my master Muḥammad b. ʿAlī al-Sanūsī ﷺ and the masters of the *Sanūsī* path ﷺ, those on the methodology of my master Ibn Idrīs ﷺ, without any alteration or changes as has been related to us and as we have witnessed. Likewise, the methodology of my master Ibrahim al-Rashid ﷺ, and my master al-Mīrghanī ﷺ, and my master al-Ahdalī ﷺ, who is closely connected to the *al-Ahdalīyya*. And all those who took from the shaykh of shaykhs, my

وَشَفِّعْ فِينَا نَبِيَّكَ سَيِّدَنَا مُحَمَّدًا صَلَّى اللهُ عَلَيْهِ وَسَلَّمَ صَاحِبَ الشَّفَاعَةِ الْعُظْمَى وَالْمَقَامَاتِ الْعَلِيَّةِ ، فَهُوَ صَلَّى اللهُ عَلَيْهِ وَسَلَّمَ الشَّفِيعُ الْمُشَفَّعُ مَرْفُوعُ الذِّكْرِ وَالْجَاهِ ، وَاسْتُرْنَا بِسَتْرِكَ الْجَمِيلَ ، يَا مَنْ أَظْهَرَ الْجَمِيلَ ، وَسَتَرَ الْقَبِيحَ بِرَحْمَتِهِ السَّرْمَدِيَّةِ ، وَلَا تَفْضَحْنَا اللَّهُمَّ فِي أَنْفُسِنَا وَلَا فِي أَهْلِينَا ، وَلَا فِي أَصْحَابِنَا يَا مَنْ لَا رَبَّ غَيْرُهُ ، وَلَا مَعْبُودَ سِوَاهُ ،

وَنَعُوذُ بِكَ اللَّهُمَّ مِنَ الْهَمِّ وَالْحَزَنِ وَالْعَجْزِ وَالْكَسَلِ وَالْجُبْنِ وَالْبُخْلِ وَغَلَبَةِ الدَّيْنِ وَقَهْرِ الرِّجَالِ وَالْأَهْوَاءِ النَّفْسِيَّةِ ، وَنَعُوذُ بِكَ اللَّهُمَّ مِنْ زَوَالِ النِّعْمَةِ ، وَفُجَاءَةِ النِّقْمَةِ ، وَضِيقِ الصَّدْرِ ، وَسُوءِ الْمُنْقَلَبِ وَعُقْبَاهُ ، وَنَسْأَلُكَ اللَّهُمَّ مِنْ كُلِّ خَيْرٍ سَأَلَكَ مِنْهُ سَيِّدُنَا مُحَمَّدٌ صَلَّى اللهُ عَلَيْهِ وَسَلَّمَ خَيْرُ الْبَرِيَّةِ ، وَنَعُوذُ بِكَ اللَّهُمَّ مِنْ كُلِّ شَرٍّ اسْتَعَاذَكَ مِنْهُ سَيِّدُنَا مُحَمَّدٌ صَلَّى اللهُ عَلَيْهِ وَسَلَّمَ رَسُولُ اللهِ ،

وَانْشُرِ اللَّهُمَّ الطَّرِيقَةَ الْأَحْمَدِيَّةَ الْإِدْرِيسِيَّةَ فِي سَائِرِ الْبِقَاعِ الْأَرْضِيَّةِ ، عَلَى نَهْجِ ابْنِ إِدْرِيسَ رَضِيَ اللهُ عَنْهُ النَّهْجِ الَّذِي تُحِبُّهُ وَتَرْضَاهُ ، فَطَرِيقُنَا الْكِتَابُ وَالسُّنَّةُ وَالدُّرُوسُ الْعِلْمِيَّةُ وَتِلَاوَةُ الْقُرْآنِ وَالْأَوْرَادِ وَالْإِكْثَارُ مِنْ ذِكْرِ اللهِ ، وَعَلَى طَرِيقِ سَيِّدِي مُحَمَّدِ بْنِ عَلِيٍّ السَّنُوسِيِّ رَضِيَ اللهُ عَنْهُ ، وَالسَّادَةِ السَّنُوسِيَّةِ ، الَّذِينَ كَانُوا عَلَى نَهْجِ سَيِّدِي ابْنِ إِدْرِيسَ رَضِيَ اللهُ عَنْهُ مِنْ غَيْرِ تَبْدِيلٍ وَلَا تَغْيِيرٍ ، كَمَا رُوِيَ لَنَا ذَلِكَ وَشَاهَدْنَاهُ ، وَعَلَى نَهْجِ سَيِّدِي إِبْرَاهِيمَ الرَّشِيدِ رَضِيَ اللهُ عَنْهُ ،

master Ibn Idrīs ﷺ, those who extended their hands to him and took him as their Shaykh and were pleased with him.

And O Allāh be pleased with all of our brothers who are traveling this path, from those who preceded us and those present with us. And shower upon them the perceptible and spiritual lights. And bind their hearts with affection, love, correct belief, mutual assistance and mutual brotherhood.

O Allāh forgive the compiler of these words and his parents, his teachers, those who accompanied him with sincere intention, and all the Muslim men and women, whether they are alive or have passed on. O my Lord, forgive and have mercy, for you are the best of those who show mercy, O Allāh.

O Allāh send blessings, peace and abundance on our liege and master, Muḥammad, the best of creation, and on his family, in every glance and breath, as many times as all that is contained in the knowledge of Allāh.

This book was completed on the 27th night of *Rajab*, 1388 AH (1968 CE), at the noble Masjid al-Azhar.

وَسَيِّدِى الْمِيرْغَنِيِّ رَضِيَ اللهُ عَنْهُ ، وَسَيِّدِى الأَهْدَلِيِّ ذِى النِّسْبَةِ الْأَهْدَلِيَّةِ ، وَكُلِّ مَنْ أَخَذَ عَنْ شَيْخِ الشُّيُوخِ سَيِّدِى ابْنِ إِدْرِيسَ رَضِيَ اللهُ عَنْهُ ، وَمَدَّ يَدَهُ إِلَيْهِ، وَاتَّخَذَهُ شَيْخًا وَارْتَضَاهُ ،

وَارْضَ اللَّهُمَّ عَنْ جَمِيعِ إِخْوَانِنَا السَّالِكِينَ لِهَذِهِ الطَّرِيقَةِ مِمَّنْ سَبَقَنَا وَمِمَّنْ حَضَرَ مَعَنَا وَأَنْزِلْ عَلَيْهِمُ الْأَنْوَارَ الْحِسِّيَّةَ وَالْمَعْنَوِيَّةَ ، وَأَلِّفْ بَيْنَ قُلُوبِهِمْ بِالْمَوَدَّةِ وَالْمَحَبَّةِ وَحُسْنِ الْعَقِيدَةِ وَالتَّعَاوُنِ وَالْمُوَالَاةِ ، وَاغْفِرِ اللَّهُمَّ لِجَامِعِ هَذِهِ الْكَلِمَاتِ وَلِوَالِدَيْهِ وَلِمَشَايِخِهِ ، وَلِمَنْ صَحِبَهُ بِحُسْنِ النِّيَّةِ ، وَلِجَمِيعِ الْمُسْلِمِينَ وَالْمُسْلِمَاتِ الْأَحْيَاءِ مِنْهُمْ وَالْأَمْوَاتِ ، رَبِّ اغْفِرْ وَارْحَمْ وَأَنْتَ خَيْرُ الرَّاحِمِينَ يَا اللهُ ،

﴿اللَّهُمَّ صَلِّ وَسَلِّمْ وَبَارِكْ عَلَى سَيِّدِنَا وَمَوْلَانَا مُحَمَّدٍ خَيْرِ الْبَرِيَّةِ،
وَعَلَى آلِهِ فِي كُلِّ لَمْحَةٍ وَنَفَسٍ عَدَدَ مَا وَسِعَهُ عِلْمُ اللهِ﴾

وَكَانَ الْخَتَامُ فِي لَيْلَةِ السَّابِعِ وَالعِشْرِينَ مِنْ رَجَبَ سَنَةَ أَلْف وَثَلَاثَمَائَة وَثَمَانَ وَثَمَانِينَ ه

APPENDICES

Appendix 1

الصَلَاةُ العَظِيمِيَّةُ

اللَّهُمَّ اِنِّي أَسْأَلُكَ بِنُورِ وَجْهِ اللهِ العَظِيمِ ، الَّذِي مَلَأَ أَرْكَانَ عَرْشِ اللهِ العَظِيمِ، وَ قَامَتْ بِهِ عَوَالِمُ اللهِ العَظِيمِ ، أَنْ تُصَلِّي عَلَى مَوْلَانَا مُحَمَّدٍ ذِي القَدْرِ العَظِيمِ ، وَ عَلَى آلِ نَبِيِّ اللهِ العَظِيمِ ، بِقَدْرِ عَظَمَةِ ذَاتِ اللهِ العَظِيمِ ، فِي كُلِّ لَمْحَةٍ وَ نَفَسٍ عَدَدَمَا فِي عِلْمِ اللهِ العَظِيمِ، صَلَاةً دَائِمَةً بِدَوَامِ اللهِ العَظِيمِ ، تَعْظِيمًا لِحَقِّكَ يَا مَوْلَانَا يَا مُحَمَّدُ يَا ذَا الخُلُقِ العَظِيمِ ، وَ سَلِّمْ عَلَيهِ وَ عَلَى آلِهِ مِثْلَ ذَلِكَ ، وَ اجْمَعْ بَيْنِي وَ بَيْنَهُ كَمَا جَمَعْتَ بَيْنَ الرُّوحِ وَ النَّفْسِ ظَاهِرًا وَ بَاطِنًا يَقَظَةً وَ مَنَامًا وَ اجْعَلْهُ يَا رَبِّ رُوْحًا لِذَاتِي مِنْ جَمِيعِ الوُجُوهِ فِي الدُنْيَا قَبْلَ الأَخِرَةِ يَا عَظِيمُ

AL-ṢALĀT AL-ʿAẒĪMIYYA

Allāhumma innī as'aluka bi-nūri wajhillāhil ʿaẓīm, al-ladhī mala'a arkāna ʿarshillāhil ʿaẓīm, wa qāmat bihī ʿawālimullāhil ʿaẓīm, an tuṣallī ʿalā mawlānā Muḥammadin dhil-qadril ʿaẓīm, wa ʿalā āli nabiyyillāhil ʿaẓīm, bi-qadri ʿaẓamati dhātillāhil ʿaẓīm, fī kulli lamḥatin wa nafasin ʿadada mā fī ʿilmillāhil ʿaẓīm, ṣalātan dā'imatan bi-dawāmillāhil ʿaẓīm, taʿẓīman li-ḥaqqika yā mawlānā yā Muḥammad yā dhal-khuluqil ʿaẓīm, wa sallim ʿalayhi wa ʿalā ālihī mithla dhālik, wajmaʿ baynī wa-baynahū kamā jamaʿta baynarrūḥi wannafsi, ẓāhiran wa bāṭinan, yaqdhatan wa manāman, wajʿalhu yā Rabbi rūḥan li-dhātī min jamīʿil wujūhi, fiddunyā qablal ākhirati, yā ʿaẓīm

THE PRAYER OF MAJESTY

O Allāh, I ask You by the Light of the Countenance of Allāh, the Majestic. Which filled the pillars of the Throne of Allāh, the Majestic. And by it are upheld the worlds of Allāh, the Majestic. That You send blessings upon our Master Muḥammad possessor of magnificent worth, and upon the family of the Prophet of Allāh, the Majestic, as much as the greatness of the Essence of Allāh, the Majestic. In every glance and in every breath, as numerous as that is contained within the Knowledge of Allāh, the Majestic. A prayer that is perpetual in the perpetuity of Allāh, the Majestic. In magnification of your worth, O our Master, O Muḥammad, O possessor of exalted character. And send peace upon him and his family just as much, and join him with me, just as You joined the soul with the nafs, outwardly and inwardly, in wakefulness and in sleep. And make him, O Lord, a soul for my body in every aspect, in the here and now, before the next world to come, O Majestic One.

MERIT OF AL-ṢALĀT AL-ʿAẒIMĪYYA

Shaykh Ibrāhīm al-Rashīd, one of the main students and successors of al-Sayyid Aḥmad b. Idrīs wrote in a letter: "As for the ʿAẓimīyya, the Messenger of Allāh ﷺ was asked about its virtues. He said: 'It outweighs *Dalāʾil al-Khayrāt* by a thousand thousand thousand thousand thousand thousand thousand times.' He said "a thousand" twenty times; and it is greater and more than that, but this is to make it easier for us to understand. We must strive to understand the secret of his saying: "in every glance and every breath, as many times as all that is contained in the infinite knowledge of Allāh, the Great."

Appendix 2

Our master, Shaykh Ṣāliḥ al-Jaʿfarī, gives in his book, The Urgent Provision for the Idle Souls, 17 reflections on the phrase, "and join him with me, just as You joined the soul with the *nafs*, outwardly and inwardly, in wakefulness and in sleep." from the prayer on the Prophet ﷺ of Shaykh Aḥmad b. Idrīs ؓ, known as al-Ṣalāt al-ʿAẓīmiyya.

ONE

This is a joining of rectification, as the soul (ruḥ) rectifies the ego (nafs) after their joining. Allāh says, "Successful is the one who purifies it."[2] From the meanings of this, and Allāh knows best, is successful is the one who purifies his nafs by his ruḥ when the lights of his ruḥ overcome his desires for the darkness of the ego and its passions.

TWO

A joining that protects from punishment as Allāh says, "Allāh will not punish them while you are among them." From the meaning of this, and Allāh knows best, while you are with them, just like His saying, "among you is the Messenger of Allāh," meaning with you

2 Qurʾān 91:9

is the Messenger of Allāh, and this general 'with-ness' includes the forms of joining which has come to you previously.

THREE

The joining of knowledge and wisdom, as Allāh says, "He teaches them the book and the wisdom."[3]. This is obtained by means of the Muḥammadan Light. My shaykh, Shaykh al-Shinqīṭī, said, "The Bedouin coming from the desert would see the light of the face of the Prophet ﷺ, then they would speak with wisdom." The Shaykh then mentioned a line of poetry from the scholars of Shinqīṭ praising the companions of the Prophet ﷺ: "The light of the Prophet enriched them from denigration...The well-bred horses are not like the lame mules". The Sufis say, from this aspect, is the question of the Bedouin to the Prophet ﷺ about his camel, should he leave it untethered and rely on Allah or tether it and rely on Allāh? By means of the Muḥammadan light he knew how to ask and [understood] that whether taking the means or not taking the means, neither are free from reliance upon Allāh.

FOUR

The joining of purification as Allāh says, "and purify them." From the meanings of this, and Allāh knows best, is purification of the ruḥ by the ruḥ, in the realms of pre-eternal joining which he remembers.

3 Qur'ān 2:129

FIVE

The joining of Prophetic avidity for the ruḥ of the believer and it is general and specific. The intention here is specific, especially for those who have taken the Aḥmadiyya spiritual path, such that their shaykh (al-Sayyid Aḥmad b. Idrīs) has turned over the responsibility of care, spiritual upbringing, refinement, guidance, concern and preservation to the Prophet ﷺ. Perhaps, this is the unique quality of this ṭarīqa, which is why its founder (Shaykh Aḥmad b. Idrīs) says: "This ṭarīqa of ours is the Muḥammadan Ṭarīqa ... This ṭarīqa of ours is the Book and the sunna."

SIX

The joining of value, and it is the primary point, by means of joining with the most precious ﷺ. He is the most perfect, the most excellent, the most virtuous, the most beautiful, the most knowledgeable, the most noble, the most honorable, the loftiest, the bravest, the most beneficial, the kindest, the most scrupulous, the most righteous, the best, the purist, the gentleness, the first, the last, and all of this enters in the meaning of His statement , "from the best of you"[4] based on the reading with a 'fattah' on the 'fa'.

SEVEN

The joining of honor based on the meaning of His statement "There has come to you a messenger from yourselves, weighty ('azīz)..." from the meanings of "'azīz" is that he ﷺ has no peer and that he is

4 Qur'ān 9:128

the one who cannot be overcome. The one who obtains this joining surpasses the peers of his time and no enemy will overcome him by Allāh's permission.

EIGHT

The joining of the Muḥammadan kindness, which is in His statement, "With the believers he is kind," so the Muḥammadan kindness engulfs him and there is no comparison for the Muḥammadan kindness in this worldly creation.

NINE

The joining of mercy which is in His statement, "With the believers he is kind and merciful."[5]. Also, in His saying, "So by mercy from Allāh, you were lenient with them." This is a special mercy, as for the general mercy it's in His statement, "We have not sent you except as a mercy to all the worlds." So, he joins with you in the joining of two mercies, general and special. And he encompasses you like two wings of a bird flying with them in the wondrous, amazing gardens of the blessed breezes of the Muḥammadan mercy. Just as our shaykh, Abu'l Muṭṭ'alib, the father of ʿAbd al-ʿĀlī, possessor of precious knowledge, al-Sayyid Aḥmad b. Idrīs, indicated to in his saying, "He is the tongue of the mercy of my essence, as for me, he recites in every direction of the creation the verse of unrestricted divine mercy." "My mercy encompasses everything."[6]

---

5 Qurʾān 9:128

6 Qurʾān 7:156

TEN

The joining of witnessing, as he ﷺ is the witness for you on the Day of Judgement of your obedience and good deeds, and they are the greatest witnesses on your behalf.

ELEVEN

The joining of glad tidings which you obtain from him ﷺ in every joining, whether in a state of wakefulness or sleep. This glad tiding is special for those who Allāh has said about them, "For them is glad tidings in this life and the Hereafter."[7]. As for the general glad tiding, it is in His saying, "Give the believers glad tidings, that for them is a great bounty from Allāh.". And in His saying "Give glad tidings to My servants, those who hear a statement and follow the best of it."[8]. So, the general and special glad tidings will be with you, elevating you, removing the thirst by the arrival of the sweet watering spring.

TWELVE

The joining of warning which is in His statement, "a warner"[9]. The light of his majesty will warn you from disobeying his statements. He ﷺ is the possessor of the encompassing beauty and majesty, as my master ʿUmar b. al-Fārid says, "His beauty is the veil for his majesty …He loves and finds sweetness there."

---

7 Qurʾān 10:64

8 Qurʾān 39:17-18

9 Qurʾān 33:46

THIRTEEN

The joining of illumination, which illumines your heart and is lit by his lamp. That is in His statement "an illuminating lamp"[10], meaning the extinguished lamps of the hearts are lit by his lamp. And by it, the earth of your body shines by the light of its Lord as al-Sayyid Aḥmad b. Idrīs says, "The earth of my body shines by the light of its Lord and He places the Book which Allāh has not left out anything from it of essential theophanies," and this book is not recited except by means of the Muḥammadan light. And the meaning here is spiritual knowledge (*al-ʿilm al-ladunnī*) through the Muḥammadan means.

FOURTEEN

The joining of the tremendous character, as in His saying "Indeed you are of a tremendous character."[11]. The one who joins with his tremendous character, that which he earns of good character, flows from him ﷺ like the diffusion of water in the branches of the tree. By that he will be characterized with the *Muḥammadan Muṣṭafawiyyan* character.

FIFTEEN

The joining of Divine allegiance as in His saying, "Indeed those who pledged allegiance with you have only pledged allegiance with

10 Qurʾān 33:47

11 Qurʾān 68:4

Allāh, Allāh's hand is over their hands." [12]. He obtains for you the virtue of allegiance whenever you shake his hand in any one of the types of joining. Here is the experiential witnessing for the masters of hearts. This is only comprehended by hearts, not written in papers. It only descends from the Master of creation onto the hearts of those who He is pleased with. As this is a protected secret and a guarded treasure. It is the secret of His saying, "Indeed those who pledged allegiance with you have only pledged allegiance with Allāh," meaning it is as if you pledged allegiance with Allāh.

SIXTEEN

The joining of uprightness (*istiqāma*), which is in His statement, "So go straight, as you have been commanded, (you) and whoever repents with you, and do not be inordinate…" So, the secret of uprightness is obtained for you by the Muḥammadan path without any deviation and no excessiveness. The meaning here is as the Precious Quṭb, al-Sayyid Aḥmad b. Idrīs, has said, "so that I am on a firm footing which doubt does not cause it to waver from any angle."

SEVENTEEN

He obtains the joining of realizing the theophanies in actions, which is in His saying "It was not you who threw, when you threw, but it was Allāh Who threw."[13]. As our beloved shaykh al-Sayyid Aḥmad b. Idrīs said [in a supplication], "so that I don't see in myself, anything, or in no-thing other than You."

---

12 Qur'ān 48:15

13 Qur'ān 8:17

Made in the USA
Middletown, DE
13 February 2025

71184313R00102